Farn

CW00348412

Tales

My escapades before, during and after World War 11

By Maurice Goss

Edited by Peter and Sylvie Goss

FOREWARD

Family and friends always knew my Father as a great story- teller. He began writing down some of these memories of his childhood in his late seventies. He initially wrote them out longhand, self -conscious of his writing because he had to a large extent 'not engaged with education' at school. My Mother Joy Goss typed these stories on an electric typewriter. Later the originals were carefully burnt.

My mother assisted my father initially in researching and organising his writings. Our regret is that the stories were not published before both my parents died in 2016.

Sylvie and I spent time revising and editing his adventures. Having no previous experience of editing and publishing, it has been a big learning curve for us both.

We would like to thank their friends, Gloria for her contribution with typing some of the stories and to Don for his contribution of old photographs. Most of all thanks to my Father for sharing his childhood stories which give us an opportunity to have a glimpse of the very different lives of a previous generation, enabling us to enjoy his childhood escapades.

DECEMBER 2018

INTRODUCTION   5

PART ONE: CALVERTON, STONY STRATFORD   9

BIRTH 15TH MARCH 1928   9
I GO TO SCHOOL 1933   10
BACK TO SCHOOL   14
CALVERTON SCHOOL   15
AVOIDING EDUCATION   16
ANGELS IN THE CHOIR   17
SUMMER HOLIDAYS 1938   19
A WINTER'S NIGHT 1938   21
SCHOOL MUSIC LESSONS   22
LAPLAND FARM 1938   25
MEMORIES OF TRADE IN THE VILLAGE   27
FELLING OF THE ELMS   30
THE DAY OF THE HUNT 1930'S   31
WAR EXPECTED   1939   33
EVACUEES 1939   35
VANDALS AT THE VICARAGE   37
WAR IS DECLARED   39
I'VE GOT SIXPENCE, OR HAVE I?   41
THE MUMMERS 1940   42
A DAY OUT – AGED 12   43
THE AIR FIELD   46
A BIG BANG   46
THE HIGHWAYMAN - FINDING A GUN – 1941   48
THE NEW GOALIE   51
BRIEF ENCOUNTER   52
MY RABBIT SKIN GLOVES 1941   54
WILD FOOD ENTERPRISE   56
BLACKBERRIES AND UNEXPECTED WORDS   58
CRICKET 1940/41   60
CATCHING RABBITS - MY POCKET MONEY   60
THE HORTONS AND CIGARETTES   62
YOUNG FARMERS' CLUB AT BLETCHLEY PARK   64
THE MOTORBIKE   66
MY FIRST PAID WORK 1940   66
OLD TIME GRAFFITI - AND A NEW PUPPY   67
HAYMAKING 1940   69
HAYMAKING WITH TOM GOODGER   70
HARVEST 1942 (AGE 13)   71

SOME OF MY DAYS THRESHING   72
WHITEHOUSE FARM   75
THRESHING AT SHENLEY DENS 1941   77
MR. COX   79
RELUCTANT ARTIST   79
TROUBLE BREWING   81
LEAVING CALVERTON   82
OUT INTO THE WORLD   84

PART TWO: MARSH GIBBON BUCKINGHAMSHIRE 1942   85

EXILE IN AYLESBURY   85
MY FIRST YEAR AT MARSH GIBBON MARCH 1942   86
THE WORKING DAY: NEVER TAKE YOUR BOOTS OFF TILL THE SUN
SETS   88
                                                                     90
THE MAN FROM THE MINISTRY   90
THERE'S ALWAYS SOMETHING TO DO   91
A BUNGLING BURGLAR   92
MORE MINISTRY MEDDLING   93
WORD OF HOME.   93
RETURN VISIT 1943   94

PART THREE: A WESTON UNDERWOOD MISCELLANY   97

THE FARMS OF WESTON UNDERWOOD   97

PHEASANT'S NEST   97
SHEARING AT COWPER'S OAK FARM 1943   101
JACK'S TAMWORTH PIGS   104
HIGGINS LODGE FARM   105
JOHN DIGBY: GREENWAYS   106
AUSTIN GRAVES: CHURCH AND PARK FARMS   107
HUNGARY HALL FARM 1942   108
PASTURES NEW SPRING 1945   116
                                                                    117
NEW PONY AND FLOAT   117
THE SCAPEGOATS: VJ NIGHT   118
A WESTON CHARACTER: "POACHER" TURNS GAMEKEEPER   129

THE WEATHER 1947   131
JUST A HOLE IN A FIELD   133
POST WAR CRICKET AT WESTON UNDERWOOD 1946   134
PLAYING THE MERCHANT TAYLOR BOYS   136
THE LAVENDER MEN   137

Introduction

When asked what he would do if he won a lot of money, my Father replied, "I would probably carry on farming until it was all gone". There is an element of truth in this statement: Maurice was working on farms all his life and I can't really imagine what else he would have done. From an early age he was working on his parents' smallholding and being sent off to family and neighbours' farms to help out. The largely agricultural communities relied on mutual aid during the difficult years of the 1930s and 1940s.

These stories are about the life of a country boy growing up before, during and after the Second World War in Calverton, Marsh Gibbon and Weston Underwood, which were then in the county of Buckinghamshire. They were written down over the last ten or so years of his life, in carefully formed copperplate italic, which Mum, and later family and friends, typed up so that he could destroy the originals.

Maurice was born in 1928 and died in 2016. He was the third child of seven children. During his early life his parents, Stanley and Ethel, were smallholder tenants in the village of Calverton, Buckinghamshire.

An unforeseen consequence of Hitler's ambitions in Europe was that fewer questions were asked about how often useful farm boys attended school. Maurice took full advantage of this, preferring to be in the working world.

His family moved from their farm in Calverton due to the land being requisitioned by the war office in 1940. The family found a farm in Weston Underwood, near Olney where two hundred years previously John Newton was the Vicar, William Cowper wrote his rural poetry and where later, pancake races originated.

They were initially tenants, the landlord owning a number of farms in the area. The relationship was not a smooth one and things came to a head after the mysterious disappearances of a redundant pump and other scrap metal. Stanley was given the choice to buy the farm or get out. Maurice spent the next week in frustration as his father weighed up the pros and cons before deciding to take out a mortgage.

The purchase of Woodlands Farm gave the family more security. Gradually their children married and left home apart from Maurice with his wife Joy and brother John and his wife Evelyn. Stanley and Ethel spent their retirement years in Olney. Stanley remained active as a local councillor and became a member of the Olney Bowls Club.

During the seventies, Maurice took over ownership of the farm, now my two brothers run it. They are the third generation of the Goss family to live at Woodlands Farm

The villages Dad describes may still look similar, and probably tidier and in better repair than in the middle of the century, but the villages in these stories are a world and a generation apart from the highly desirable commuter suburbs they are now.

When he arrived in Weston Underwood, there were nearly twenty men at a meeting of the National Union of Farmworkers; now there are few, if any, all year-round farm labourers in the village. A family with seven children occupied what is now a third of a "cottage". Dad said, for good or bad, everyone knew everyone's business and who they were related to, who they voted for and how much they earned. Going round the local pubs was better than the music hall. You got to know everyone, and everyone knew you. I can testify that we've been to some unlikely places and been greeted with "Hello, Maurice!" from someone.

Apart from farming, Maurice had a lifelong love of cricket, and a great interest in local and family history. Mum and Dad traced his family back to 1596 in the mid-Bucks villages his parents came from. They also found much about Weston history and Cowper's life there. He still had a liking for some opera, particularly the tenor Beniamino Gigli, singing being the one thing that he seemed to enjoy at school.

There were some tales told to me that were not written down, vague in my memory; I should have recorded them and taken more notice. I expect every family has its stories, legends and traditions, these help us to understand our relatives and how they lived -perhaps we can be more tolerant and understanding as we find out about their lives. It is certain that we owe gratitude to our forebears for their struggles, hard work and determination, trying to make a better world for future generations.

Peter Goss
December 2018

Calverton Village

Part One: Calverton, Stony Stratford

Birth 15th March 1928

I was born in the hamlet of Upper Weald, Calverton, on one of the impoverished smallholdings in the time of the farming depression of the twenties and thirties.

Soon after my arrival into the world, my Gramma Goss, the matriarch of the family, came to inspect the new infant. After taking a good look at me she turned to mother and said, "You'll never rear that one, Ethel!"

Despite this unpromising beginning, I started writing this in 2006 and these are some reflections and adventures of my early life.

Where I was born Upper Weald

I go to school   1933

School began for me after Easter 1933 at St. Mary's Church School for Girls, which also catered for all infants up to the age of seven. The building is now a public house, (The Plough).

The Headmistress was Mrs. Plum, assisted by her daughter, Ada. Our infant teachers were Miss. Horn, a kind, friendly teacher in class one; class two was governed by Enid Wormald, an older, stricter lady, any misdemeanours being punished by smacks with a ruler on hands or legs.

I settled well in Class One and enjoyed it, until suddenly, my first year was interrupted.

Infant classes ended at 3.30pm, giving village children half an hour unsupervised wait for the bus to take them home. We would often go to the yard in front of the

cinema; this led to an unfortunate accident for me.
From there I saw the new Christmas display in the Co-op window, ran over the road to investigate, and was hit by a car travelling at speed, coming down the London Road.

I did not see the car but still remember being in the air above the bonnet before I fell into the road outside Canvin's butcher's shop into which I was carried and placed on the chopping block.

I was soon aware of a large number of faces gawping at the poor wretch lying on the marble slab. The arrival of Dr Habgood put a stop to the peep show as he had the blinds drawn.

The Doctor fitted temporary splints before the Wolverton Works ambulance took me to hospital at Northampton, where I would stay for a several weeks.

On Christmas morning the Mayor of Northampton and other dignitaries visited the children's ward, giving each child an orange and three new pennies of 1934. They spent some time at my bed- whether sympathetic or just curious I don't know. I had a trellis construction above my bed from which was suspended a rope and a pulley with a lead weight on one side as a counterweight to keep a much damaged, plastered leg hanging above the bed.

Mother visited often. It must have been difficult with the family at home to look after. There were already three younger than me and Audrey a little older, and Basil to worry about. She had to bike to Stony Stratford to catch the bus to Northampton.

When during the time I was there the ward was in isolation for ten days and visitors were not allowed inside the ward, the beds were pushed to the entrance to the ward and visitors, six at a time, looked through the glass and waved to us children.

After the main hospital, I was sent to a convalescent home in Dallington, a large impressive house. I was on the upper storey. It had a large balcony on to which we were pushed each day and left- no doubt very nice in the summer, but this was the end of February. This harsh remedy worked. I was home in time for my sixth birthday in the middle of March.

Not a very auspicious start to my education!

Below is the Bucks Standard report on this incident. The exact date is unknown but It would be 1933.

(From The Bucks Standard, date unknown)

An unfortunate accident befell a schoolboy named Goss as he was attempting to cross the main road near the Calverton Road junction to the High Street on Tuesday afternoon. He was knocked down by a motor-car and sustained a fractured thigh, a lacerated left ankle, and cuts to the face and legs. He was attended by Dr. A.H. Habgood and conveyed by the Wolverton Works motor ambulance to the Northampton General Hospital. He is a son of Mr. and Mrs. Goss of Upper Weald, Calverton, and his brother some time ago met with a similar accident, from which he has not yet recovered.

(This refers to brother Basil, left with a limp after a similar accident in the same place.)

Back to School

My second school, St Giles for Boys, was in the High Street of Stony Stratford – a tall, imposing brick building of three storeys- Hooton's Bazaar at number 32 had the ground floor, the school had the top two storeys with the entrance round the back.

The thing I remember most was the intense cold in the winter: the fish tank in the classroom had ice on it. We did exercises for half an hour before lessons to try to get warm. The only refreshment we had was a hot beaker of Horlicks mid-morning. Eventually, we had a welcome respite when the toilets froze, and we were given two weeks holiday.

The classes were Standards. In Standard 1, I survived Miss Hussey; then Standard 2, I tolerated the Headmaster, Mr. W.J. Toms (Puffing Billy); in Standard 3, I suffered under Mr. Cheeseman (Cheddar).
He said that I had little inclination or talent for classwork" – I think he was right.

I was to meet both Mr. Toms and Mr. Cheeseman again at the New School.

Family Picture Maurice at front in braces

Calverton School

Calverton school was closed in 1924 by Bucks Education Committee, who gave a written undertaking to convey Calverton children to schools in Stony Stratford, this being the condition of closing.

After the summer term of 1939, the bus service was withdrawn, leaving nearly forty children to walk to school from Upper Weald; this was three miles each way.

Our parents, led by our Rector, Rev Ravenscroft, refused to send us to school so when September came, and term began, no bus- no school.

Our Rector wrote many letters on our behalf, mostly to D.E. Cooke The Education Secretary pointing out the danger of children as young as five walking up to three miles each way in the winter.

There was a stalemate until November when the bus service resumed. I had had three months off to advance my "out of school education"

Maurice with siblings

Avoiding Education

In 1938 the St. Giles School closed, and we then moved on to the Council school in Russell Street where I encountered Mr. Walters, Mr. Owen and the Headmaster, Mr. Wright.

Soon after my first year, I was chosen to work in the furnace cellar; shovelling coke from the hole it was shot down from the street, over to the furnace some yards away. A dirty, dusty job that I enjoyed!

The master, Mr. Wright, soon discovered I was much more use here and was so much better with a shovel than a pen. He sent me to work in the garden where I planted, hoed and lifted potatoes, sprayed and pruned the orchard, in season. I later helped to dig the air raid shelter. Throughout this time, I maintained a lowly position in class and duly failed all exams.

When the time came to go the then new school in Wolverton Road to complete my education, the rest of the children from Calverton missed the first term as the school bus was withdrawn and our parents refused to send us to school. It did not really affect me as I cycled to school, delivering milk on the way. However, I was pleased to lend my support.

News of me as a non-academic handyman preceded me to the new school. The caretaker had gone to war, the school was packed with evacuees almost doubling the numbers the school was built for, with two large classes in the corridors, so I was in great demand doing odd jobs inside and outside the school.

Mostly the teachers were good, although Headmaster Toms, a friend of my Dad, missed no chance of caning me.

One or two other boys would be called out of assembly most days to work in the garden or other work with me. With the school so crowded, I started having more and more time off to help with the haymaking. By this time the school had had enough of me and I of it.

Angels in the Choir

Soon after my tenth birthday I was conscripted into the church choir. From then on, I attended church three times every Sunday and choir practice on Tuesday night.

The week before my debut in the choir, my cassock and surplice were sent up for fitting. On my first Sunday, I was dressed at home and then walked the whole length of the village, looking like a lost penguin. Another boy from the village started at the same time. He was from a family to whom washing was alien and his usual state of clothing was not to be desired, but on this occasion, there he was on the doorstep looking very different and I heard his mother say with pride, "You look just like a little bishop".

The choir numbered about sixteen strong, sometimes more, sometimes less, as on the occasions when we were late for matins, we would buy sweets from Mrs. Cowan's shop and play in the stream until the service ended.

One hot afternoon, walking home from Sunday school, the road had been tarred and gravelled. Barrels of tar had been left on the roadside every twenty yards or so. These were to empty into a boiler on wheels and when boiling, sprayed on to the road with a kind of watering can. The gravel was then thrown on top and rolled in with a steamroller. Progress was slow, so the driver had enough time to roll it in many times and give rides to pleading village boys, but he was less keen when the whistle was blown too many times. The empty wooden barrels were left on the side of the road for collecting up later. Seeing these barrels at the top of the hill in Middle Weald, a helpful thought came to me. Two brothers from Park Road in Middle Weald were also involved in rolling the barrels into the ditch, but I thought would be easier for the workmen to collect them up later if they were all rolled to the bottom of the hill into the brook.

This was not a good idea! The tar got on my hands; face, on my hair and on my clothes. I knew I would get into trouble when I got home but did not expect the commotion that occurred.

Tea was laid on the table, but not for me. I was ushered into the scullery, water was boiled, and the bath bought from the peg on the back wall. When the water was hot, I was stripped and Mother came in with a scrubbing brush, carbolic soap and a heavy hand.

My screams bought Gwen from next door. She said her Dad had some Turps, which she used. This was fetched and tried with some success. When Dad came home from milking, he rubbed lard into my mop of hair. I don't know how so much tar got into my hair and on my face. He also used a thick metal comb, but this pulled my hair out. Eventually, I had to have a haircut but still went to school on Monday with traces of tar left in my hair.

Calverton - the route of the tar barrels

Summer Holidays 1938

Alice and Charlie Edwards and his in-laws, Mr. and Mrs. Noah Neal, lived in the adjoining cottage standing edgeways to the road close to our house. Charlie's children were Jean and Brian, a little younger than myself, but older brother Emlyn was my friend. I spent much of my time playing at the end of their long garden, amongst the fruit trees.

Charlie was away all week working in the car factory, in Oxford, Noah was not very active being an old pensioner.

One summer holiday we made a camp in their old outhouse. It was quite untidy already, so we made little extra mess. We ate picnics of rhubarb, gooseberries, onions and raw mushrooms from the paddock, quite awful.

There was a bell, hanging from an apple tree with strings to the other trees nearby. The idea was that when birds settled on the branches the bell would ring and scare them: it was quite loud. But, actually it only rang when big birds landed on the tree or when juvenile scrumpers climbed the branches.

One day I suggested that we borrow the bell, so we carefully removed it and went around the village ringing the bell and shouting, causing curiosity and even alarm amongst the cottages until the parson came by and ordered us to stop, so we had to put the bell back.

On the corner of Mr. Neil's farm was a wooden water barrel to catch the rainwater. It was held together with iron rings. That would make perfect hoops, something none of us had ever had. The barrel was nearly empty. I tipped it over and easily removed the top hoops and then stood it back in place. We had hours of fun with these hoops, up and down the roads but taking care not to go too near to the Neil's house.

Unfortunately, we kept them too long. A heavy thunderstorm filled the barrel with water and it seeped out of the sides and the top expanded so that when I tried to replace the hoops they would not fit.

Brian thought that he would be blamed for the damage, so it was time for us to move our camp to the swallow hovel where our cart was kept. This was our favourite winter spot, on our ex-army ammunition carrier wagon. We would give poor Noah a wide berth.

A Winter's Night 1938

One winter's night in1938 Dad, as usual, went off with his hurricane lamp to milk the cows.

After milking, he climbed the steps to the hayloft above to throw down hay from this uncovered area to the hayracks below. Leaving the lamps near the cows, the loft was almost total darkness. As he put the folk into the hay, he was startled by a voice saying, "Don't stab

19

me Guvnor!" A tramp was lying in the hay. Dad took him down to the light and gave him a drink of milk.

After first telling him he could stay the night, but not to smoke in the hayloft, and to be gone by morning, Dad asked him where he was from and why he was on the road.

The man said he had no money, no home and was looking for work.

Dad asked him, "Were you in the war?"

"Yes." he said, taking his discharge papers from his pocket. Soon the conversation turned to the battles of France and then Dad invited him into the house for food. I can just remember this tramp coming in before we were sent to bed. He stayed around for several days until one of Dad's ex-service friends got him a menial job in Wolverton Works and lodgings in New Bradwell.

We were a bit scared of him and did not go up into the loft in the dark for some time.

Dad told this account many times, but I never got to know the man's name or whether he stayed in the area.

Maurice's Father Stanley Goss 1914

School Music Lessons

Back after the Easter holidays, much had to change to cope with the ever-growing numbers of evacuees. An extra class was formed that Mr. Toms himself was to teach, much to my surprise I was among those, I don't know why.

I met headmaster Toms at the Boys' School and later at the New School. He never liked me, the fault was mine, I never listened to a thing he said and had no wish to be there. After the Boys' School closed, Mr. Toms became head of the new school and I went to Russell Street for a further two years.

Now I was to be reacquainted with Mr. Toms and Mr. Cheeseman. Nothing had changed. I was remembered from the previous school. This soon led to more frequent days off. I bribed Brenda so nobody at home knew.

We were shown our room, where I had never been before; Mr. Toms' influence was obvious, the grand piano taking centre stage. "Mr. Toms ran his own ship." He was a fine musician, was organist at St Giles Church and ran a fine choir. He was a lover of opera, as I was soon to discover, other lessons were second place to the master's passion for music.

We were not long in our new classroom before the first music lesson with Mr. Tomms; but first a teacher was borrowed for the mornings from Wolverton, with the object of teaching us the words of the French national anthem in French. We would sing it at the start of each lesson as a tribute to our brave allies. Very strange, had they not just surrendered without telling us, leaving our army isolated on the continent? Anyway, after a chat between the teacher and Mr. Tomms we were to use the English translation, so our French teacher would come no more.

In one lesson we had learnt La Marseillaise, we sang it well, all were pleased. It was decided that one more lesson would do then we could move on. At the second lesson we remembered and sang it well, I remember it still. "Carmen" with its rousing chorus of the "Toreadors' Song" was next. Most of the tuneful songs from Carmen were among the ones we sang.

Carmen was easy to learn, and we sang well together. All this was about to change, Mr. Toms could now turn to his real passion: Italian opera, for which mostly he had English translations. What had changed? Many of the class were uninterested by the end of the lesson. Mr. Toms, sensing the mood, asked if any of the class would rather do something else. A surprising number indicated that they would like a change, so he took their names. They got a change- they did not attend any more but were returned to class, as we all were soon to do.

As we were in a small group, our progress quickened. The first we sang was Pagliacci by Leoncavallo. I was soon singing loud and clear. There was a girl, Josie, a better singer than I, but the part needed a male singer. The down side being that I was called to the front to sing solo to the class. Me, the shy, nervous boy with no confidence- but at least I am to sing a clown, so here goes! Trembling at first,

Vesti La Giubba- " On with the motley, the paint and the powder... "

I then thought, "if I am a jester, then I will add my own bit to the part," so when I got to "Laugh, Punchinello", I laughed long and loud and then added my Charlie Chaplin impression. Everyone was laughing. I'd got away with it.

My truancy led to much punishment, not all deserved. The fact that music could heal that scar and we could work together, if only in music, was good. In our final lessons we sang bits from Tosca and Rigoletto, but it was "The Marriage of Figaro" that we struggled with, this I had to learn and sing. Mr. Toms spoke to me directly, at the end of term he called me "Maurice" and said he looked forward to having me and the other members of the class in his choir.

This had been the sole reason for the music lessons.

Now as the term ended, so did my desire to be there. Our hay was ready, so I was needed to help Dad and Mum to get it into the stack, then to help Mr. Goodger get his. The harvest would mean a month at Mr. Cowley's, and the steam thresher- I would go anywhere it went.

Lapland Farm 1938

From the age of ten I spent my Easter holiday at my uncle's farm at Brill. He lived there with my aunt Amy and their daughter, Betty, who was much older than me.

My Aunt Amy, a former schoolteacher was very good to me but quite strict. I played in the stream among the daffodils and the railway watching the trains come through the tunnel under Brill Hill.

When I was older, I was sent wooding with an old pram up in the woods, where I picked primroses, I was also taken out on the tram that ran to Quainton.

Each morning I went with Uncle Jim to feed the stock and on the way back he visited two ponds where he would take a moorhen's egg and replace it with one from his pocket with a cross on it (so that he did not take it another day). He would have these eggs for his breakfast with his bacon, cooked on a paraffin stove.

One year my sister Brenda came with me. We were sent up the woods with an old pram to fill with firewood and we were very successful. Also, this year my birthday came in the holiday. Plans were made for the party, no one else was invited, just the five of us, but Auntie would play the piano, Betty the violin. We could all sing-along and party food was made for tea- I couldn't wait.

Unfortunately, during the day came a setback- Auntie said I had piddled over the toilet seat! I would have to stand in the corner for twenty minutes while they had tea. I pleaded guilty and said it would be quite an achievement to do any other as the seat was so high. But Aunt being ever the old schoolmistress was not impressed, and I heard the jelly and blancmange and cakes being brought to the table. However, after another appeal, the sentence was reduced, and the party went ahead.

When I went home my aunt asked me to pick some cowslip and dandelion heads for her to make some wine.

This is the sort of challenge I liked; as soon as I got home, I started on the dandelions, which were already out and plentiful. I took an enamel pail with a lid, and had the help from a friend, until he got fed up. I finished on the roadside at Beachampton, eventually filling the pail with the amount she said she wanted.

The next day I took the pail to show the family, I lifted the lid, and to my disappointment they had withered and there was only half the amount, so I had to top it up every evening for the rest of the week, and then mother made a parcel and sent them to aunt Amy.

It was a fine spring and the cowslips were large and plentiful, I spent every spare minute one week until I filled the pail on Saturday, mother again packed them up and put the parcel on the bus to Aylesbury where aunt or uncle would pick them up. Later on, a 7lb jar of marmalade came especially for me as a reward.

Extended family - Maurice 2nd left back row

Memories of Trade in the Village

Returning to Calverton, in my eighties whilst walking around the village, the most obvious difference to me is the lack of life in the daytime.

During my childhood in Upper Weald, the street was always alive: with four cow herds being taken to and from the fields for milking, twice each day. Various horses and sheep and other through traffic went by. In the afternoon, the women might be seen, off with an old pram looking for wood, or black-berrying in season, when not helping on the farms.

Mr. Goss and Mr. Cowley managed each morning to take their milk churns out at the same time so discussed current events for some time- would there be another war or not?

Many of the men worked on the farms and were about all day. Some men had found work in car factories and would stay away all week, returning home for the weekends. One man became a 'rep' for Armitage Tea and went off in a Singer 8, EYY 177. Many local salesmen called in at the village.

Mr. Hall, of Hall & White, Grocers, called on Tuesdays for an order to be delivered at the end of the week. In our house, the order always began with '16lbs of sugar'. This continued until one day Mr. White called to say that Mr. Hall would not be calling again as he had died.

Mr. Calladine, a shoe repairer, called weekly. Mr. Cowley, a baker from Stony Stratford, called, with his white horse and cart. Mr. Bowman, another baker, also called. Canvin's, the butchers, came twice a week.

The International Stores delivered in such an old van that the children could run and overtake it. The Leighton Steam Laundry collected some of the village washing from those who could afford the service.

Roberts the Ironmongers' rep called. He would make ordinary conversation while drinking his mug of cocoa, then start his sales patter in a half singing, half talking voice, describing the complete content of the shop, always in the same order.

Lampitts came to collect accumulators to charge them up to run wireless sets on.

Radwells soft drinks lorry was open backed and rather a temptation to young passers by.

Mr. Keys from Horwood had a three-wheeler van built around a motorcycle; he carried general goods and confectionery, my favourite being sherbet dabs with a liquorice straw.

A turban-headed, white-bearded Indian, carrying two huge suitcases stuffed with silks, scarves and such, travelled to Wolverton by train, then walked the villages for miles around. He would open his cases almost before the door was opened, but I don't remember anyone buying much. I know he travelled many miles on foot as he called on my cousins who lived thirty miles away.

And then there was Mr. Irving, selling ice cream from his 'Stop me and buy one' bike.

Mr. Bonham came up from Stony Stratford on Sundays to help Mr. Saunders on a family smallholding. He arrived one week in a new Vauxhall 12 car, registration NV 2806. It had a chromium-fluted bonnet with bright shiny headlights. We had never seen anything like it!

Mr. Cox delivered the Sunday papers. He usually stood in the middle of the road at about one o'clock and shouted, "Papers!" Occasionally, he was delayed for two hours delivering papers to 'The Shoulder of Mutton' and Dad would sit complaining that he couldn't read the paper before milking.

Canvin Butchers of Stony Stratford – Mr Chambers (head over fence), Mrs Edwards and two daughters, son Pierce at front, became manager of Empire Cinema Wolverton, Charlie arms folded, Maurice's Godfather.

Felling of the Elms

The Elm trees around the paddock were sold to Austells of Loughborough and felled by two woodmen from Leicestershire. They slept at night on sacks of hay in the hay wagon. It was early summer, so the trees to be felled were in full leaf and when down on the ground, gave all the children a great place to play. We spent every evening climbing and hiding in the dense foliage.

By the end of the week, on Saturday in need of a change, Emlyn went to the pond at the bottom of the field. Brother John, who was about five years old at the time, followed us down to the paddock. While we were trying to reach a moorhen's nest John fell into the water, something we noted with interest but no concern.

The pond was small but joined to a larger one in Alf Saunders' field by a narrow channel. John floated through this channel under the hedge and we climbed the fence into the field to watch his progress, making no effort to save him or to raise the alarm. He could not swim but he never went under. After some minutes, he floated to the rushes at the other side of the pond, suddenly realising he might be wet and worrying what they would say at home, we helped him out and took him back.

The day of the Hunt   1930's

Audrey and I joined the young farmers when she was twelve and I was ten. The meetings were held at 10.30am on Saturday mornings at Lady Leon's, Bletchley Park. We were taken by Jean Holland, in an old car with a canvas roof and tiny windows made of celluloid that had cracked with age, making the windscreen like a cobweb.

On our way home one week we saw the hunt coming our way. Emlyn was waiting, so off we went together to open the gate. At the gateway to The Grove, a few riders threw us coppers. We usually collected two or three pence.

I knew all the fields well. In the Autumn I had had two weeks with my Dad, helping him prepare for the hunt season. We went around the fields in Whadden and Beachampton. He was paid by the hunt to take down barbed wire, where possible and to put red flags in the hedge where it had to remain.

In the spring we went around again to replace the wire and mend broken fences to fill in the gaps in the hedge with a load of posts and rails, which were provided by the hunt.

The Whaddon chase hunt was wealthy and well supported. Up to half their followers were serving officers in uniform. The hunt paid full compensation for any stock lost to the fox and at the point-to-point all the farmers and their families were given a small hamper of food and free drink.

In the thirties the hunt started a competition for the best piece of hedge laying anywhere in the area. Dad won the first prize of £25 for the first three years, after which they asked him not to compete again, but gave him two bottles of scotch for a piece of demonstration hedge laying.

On this morning, the fox was found in the Gorse Field. Mr. Cowley cleared this field at the beginning of the war. The hunt followed through the field where a stream ran through the middle. From where we watched, with my Dad and Perce Edwards, we could see the riders clear the stream. As they all jumped, one horse stopped suddenly. The rider sailed over the stream without his horse, landing on his head on the opposite bank. We all hurried to the spot where the rider lay motionless on the ground.

Dad and Perce found a gate in the field and with the help of two huntsman laid him on the gate and carried him to Fairfield Farm while another huntsman was sent to telephone for the doctor. Another went to The Shoulder of Mutton for a bottle of brandy in the hope that it might revive the injured huntsman. We went back to the scene of the accident to see if anything useful had fallen out of his pockets.

After our fruitless journey we returned to find that the doctor had pronounced the rider dead, while the brandy was being consumed by the living.

I was in the street later in the afternoon when a large Rolls Royce came along and slowed down. The chauffeur said, "Hey boy has there been an accident, someone fallen off their horse?"

"Yes!" said I. "He's at the farmhouse and he's dead!"

This bought forth a scream from the new widow seated in the back seat. Fortunately for them, my Dad came by at that moment and explained it with more tact while I later had a real telling off for my lack of compassion.

War Expected   1939

Danny Syryalt of Middle Weald came to see Dad on a Sunday morning to ask if he would sheer the sheep. It was many weeks since all other farmers' sheep had been shorn, and the plight of these poor sheep had been a topic of talk for some time. Dad, always eager to earn any money said that he would.

Monday morning, I, either on holiday or at home on some pretence, was able to help, arriving with our hand driven shears tied to Dad's bike.

The farmer showed us the sheep penned up in the yard, said that he was busy and disappeared into the house.

Having turned the handle of the shearer at home previously, I said I could do that until Mr. Syryalt came back. This I did and rolled and tied the fleece while Dad caught the next sheep. It was a much slower job than expected. The sheep were very thin and very dry. They sheared badly the cutter needed cleaning regularly and several had maggots that had to be dealt with.

After some time, several hours later, we had a rest. Dad lit his pipe, walked to the farmhouse and knocked on the door but there was no response. Dad asked me if I could do any more. I was very tired, and my arms ached from turning the handle of the machine but I would not admit it and so we went on.

In the middle of the afternoon Mr. Syryalt emerged with a bottle of beer for Dad and a bottle of lemonade for me. After being told we were going home, as I could do no more, he said he would take over for a while as if he was doing us a favour.

When we left to go home for milking, he asked Dad to see if old Sam Edward, our neighbour, would come the next day to share my job. Sam, always keen to earn enough for a trip to The Shoulder of Mutton, obliged.

Unexpectedly, the army on manoeuvres arrived and made camp in Thompson's Piece, a field in front of our farm, close to the sheep pen. This interested me much more than the sheep.

First a lorry load of troops arrived, unloaded and they began to erect large bell tents in two rows next to the road. Numbered pegs were hammered in the other side of the field, in front of the house. This organised chaos continued, until mid-day and this oversized scout camp began to take shape.

Next a convoy of lorries towing field guns arrived escorted by dispatch riders who drove each to its numbered peg. The soldiers took their kit bags to the tent. When we left all was calm and the smell of cooking filled the air. I returned after tea with the other children but the guard on the gate barred us from the field. Viewed from our house, little happened the next day, just a few exercises. No urgency.

It was just before the war, they were probably waiting to see what was going to happen.

What a difference two years later when the army was tank-training using Calverton Lane as a battlefield. The grass verges dragged out onto the road, the tarred roads damaged and tanks driving straight though hedges into the grass fields, during mock battles.

No one complained having been assured that compensation would be generous

Evacuees 1939

In July the Billeting officer came to every house to see how many evacuee children each could take. This was decided by rooms available and not on ability to look after them.

Soon the buses arrived with diamond patterned sticky tape on the darkened windows, discharging bewildered children. They were viewed with suspicion by we local boys. We wondered with what effect doubling the population was going to have on our way of life.

Revered Ravonscoft set about entertaining the children. He formed a club that met twice weekly in the schoolroom, but he would not let us local children go. He also got four boys to join the choir, which we did not like, so at the first service we sang flat so that he would think the cockneys could not sing.

The parents of the evacuees came by a "free special" train to Wolverton on Sundays to visit the children. The children were very excited but most parents, after a visit to the foster homes, quickly made their way to the Shoulder of Mutton for opening time where they remained until it closed.

After Church I joined the children who sat on the grass or played on the wall. Some of them were very distressed at seeing so little of their parents who were enjoying the day away from the stresses of London.

The Poynters were evacuees, early victims of the Blitz. They came to stay with other members of their family, already living in a small semi-detached house in Oakley Lane. So now there were two families crammed into this tiny house.

One day, Walter Poynter and family left the cottage and toured around the village looking for lodgings, but evacuees or soldiers had already taken up the houses with space. They finished up on our doorstep asking to stay in a barn.

Dad could only offer the hay barn loft – it had no facilities, just a water tap in the yard. This would do well they said. So, after said they could stay until they found a cottage and there would be no charge and he would fetch their few possessions after milking. They could also use the bathroom in our house as they wished, as the door was never locked.

Walter Poynter, his wife and children – Dennis who was about sixteen and Jean fourteen – were a nice respectable family who had unfortunately fallen on hard times. They had no work and very little money, so they lived on cheap milk straight from the cow, bread and marg and penny tins of fish paste bought by the dozen.

We children spent our spare time with Dennis and Jean. Amongst their few things they had a small tent, something we never had. We pitched it in the paddock near home for a while but then through that sunny summer moved to any field that took our fancy – no one seemed to mind.

Walter eventually got work with the Observer Corps and a house in Lower Weald so they moved out, but we still remained friends. Dennis joined the Air Training Corps and the first from this group to become a pilot. After a successful flying career, he was sadly killed in a motorcycle accident coming home on leave.

Vandals at the Vicarage

After the summer holidays, spent haymaking, I returned to a school much changed. A school of evacuees from Chingford had come to join us, filling every space. Village children were sent to Russell Street School for dinner. This led one afternoon, when returning along Vicarage Walk, to some boys entering the Vicar's garden and later some boys were seen leaving, eating fruit and with bulging pockets.

Next morning at a crowded assembly, a grim-looking headmaster, supported by the Vicar, relayed the news to all, that vandals had damaged the garden and taken pears. Village boys were responsible and would stay behind while the Chingford pupils would go to their classes. Would the boys own up? No response. He pleaded, threatened and even suggested leniency - silence. Eventually he called me to the front.

"You must know who was with you!"
"It wasn't us, Sir".
"Who was with you?"
"It wasn't us, Sir. It must have been someone else, Sir".

We were sent back to the classroom with a warning that he would get to the bottom of this and we had lost our chance of leniency and culprits would be dealt with severely.

Back in class, hoping things might calm down, I was ill prepared when our master said that three boys, I was one, would remain in at break-time to be interviewed. He just told us to empty our pockets. This led to some of my personal possessions being seized and confiscated - among them my tin containing a Rizla cigarette roller, papers and dried red clover heads, which mixed with discarded fag ends, made a dreadful concoction only the very brave among my friends would share.

Nothing came from our interview, but master knew more than we had said. He dismissed the others then dragged me by the ear to be caned by my chain-smoking Headmaster for smoking.

Village boys can be very loyal, dishonest when necessary - and I am not saying who the culprits were.

War is Declared

At the outbreak of war Dad was made air raid warden and our house was the local ARP post, we had to store stirrup pumps and buckets of sand, we were also supplied with a telephone, a real luxury.

The post was allocated No 7, each time the air raid siren sounded we would wait ten minutes to allow chief warden Toms, my Headmaster, to get to headquarters at Stony Stratford from his house in York Road, or more likely from the Conservative Club, so we could report "Post 7, manned."

Dad called a meeting in the middle of the road to discuss the building of an air raid shelter. It was agreed to build it at the bottom of our garden. Grampy Morgan, a charming old Welsh farmer living opposite, declined to help, saying that he would stand in the hollow tree in the rick yard if the bombers came. Dad tried to remind him of the fate of the trees in the Somme in the First World War, but he was adamant.

A start was made on the shelter on the following Saturday morning. People arrived with spades and barrows. The sides of an old hen house were sunk into the ground for walls. Tea was provided, and a good start was made, but enthusiasm dwindled rapidly. Before the roof was ever finished the war had ended.

Our house soon became an "an open house" when the siren sounded people came and went as they wished, some were afraid, and others came to gossip, neighbour Bates and his family of five came every night and stayed the night in our front room, they left a florin (10p) on the table every morning.

A soldier, Len Morse, and his wife Ivy, lived in one bedroom, and our family numbered eight at the time, (Brother Basil being away at work in Coventry) which meant most nights there were 16; in our three-bedroom house. How did our tea and sugar ration go around so many?

In the winter of 1940-41 Hitler, hoping to end the war quickly, bombed Calverton. Three times on different Friday nights bombs fell around us, on the first occasion four fell near our farmhouse. These were pancake bombs filled with shrapnel, leaving hollow craters. An oil bomb failed to ignite, sprayed oil all around, and then disintegrated, two weeks later two huge bombs fell in the paddock nearby which blew out every window at Fairfield Farm and left a huge pile of clay.

Upstairs in bed, we children were awoken by this huge explosion; the ceiling fell on our beds, filling the room with dust and five children rushed downstairs. Dad went out to our buildings and found the three horses very agitated, he went to the field to calm then and they led him straight to the bombsite.

While mother's attention was elsewhere, Audrey and I slipped out to see how many houses had been damaged but, meeting up with Dad he said he had found where all the bombs had dropped, and all the houses were standing; a very lucky escape. The third raid: incendiaries. These fell in Lower Weald and started several fires where they had hit houses but were soon put out with stirrup pumps. Nevertheless, this caused quite a panic in the village.

When father went to investigate, he found some of the villagers leaving their houses to hide in the ditch, fearing the Germans would see the fires and come with high explosives.

For us children bombing on Friday night was very convenient. It meant that we were the first on the scene on Saturday morning, collecting our souvenirs to trade at school the following week. I found a fin that guided one of the bombs. I swapped it for an old green federal bicycle, shrapnel I exchanged for cigarette cards and a pocket watch that did not work.

I've got Sixpence, or Have I?

Ordinary life went on, we sold three shorthorn heifers to Joe Towfield. On Saturday morning, I helped drive them to the next village to a field near Whaddon. For this I was given as pay a silver three-penny piece.

On the way home from this lucrative job I unfortunately decided to do a handstand up against a telegraph pole and lost my money. I have not to this day been able to locate it.

However, fortune smiled on me that weekend. The next morning the heifers were back in our field so we again drove them to Whaddon, this time to a field a little further away with better fences. This time I was given three pennies and by remaining upright, I took them home.

Stony Stratford.   High Street.

The Mummers 1940

The Rector announced from the pulpit the date of the children's Christmas party. After the tea and before the Adults Concert the Rector said he would like the children to perform an ancient play he had discovered, called "The Mummers" and he requested that any children who would like to take part remain after the service.

Only six boys from the choir were interested, for six of the parts and a girl was recruited, so the cast of seven was complete.

The Rector read the short text. As soon as he was finished, I jumped up! "Please can I be St. George" The Rector said he would consider who would be best suited for each part – this I knew meant "NO."

After a few more minutes we were given our parts, mine turned out to be Beelzebub. I entered into the spirit of the play and spent the next playtimes at school sitting on my own repeating the lines.

On the eventful day we had a good tea, but then my evening got off to a bad start. Fooling around when I should have been helping to move the tables. I knocked over an empty chair next to the one the Rector sat on and on which he had left his open tobacco tin. The contents were scattered all over the floor as the tin rolled. The Rector was furious and turned bright red, all salvage attempts were futile.

The play went ahead with a group of hideously dressed children rushing around the stage. I tripped up the steps and after the initial stage fright, gabbled through my few lines. That was the end of any thespian aspirations I may have had.

> [Enter Moll Dorothy.]
> In comes old Moll Dorothy,
> With her black face, and good morrow to ye.
> (Sweeps a space for performance.)
>
> [Enter Father Christmas.]
> Here comes Father Christmas, welcome or welcome not.
> I hope old Father Christmas never will be forgot;
> I've a little time to tarry, and a short time to stay,
> And show you a little sport before I go away.
>
> [Enter Paynim Knight.]
> In comes I, with sword in hand,
> Where is the man that dares to bid me stand ?
> I would cut him and hew him as small as flies,
> And send him to h—— to make mince pies.
>
> [Enter St. George.]
> In comes Saint George, with sword in hand.
> I am the man that dares to bid you stand ;
> I am the man, thou Turkish knight,
> I came to Turkeyland to fight.
> I fought the dragon. and brought him to the slaughter,
> And then I married the King of Egypt's daughter.
> A battle! a battle! between you and I,
> To see which on the ground shall lie.
> (They fight with swords ; the Knight is wounded.)
>
> [Enter the Jolly Doctor.]
> In comes the Jolly Doctor. I can cure the pix, the pox, the palsy,
> and the gout.
> All pains within, all pains without.
> Where's your pain lie, master? (examines). So, so, so,
> It's between the top of his head and the end of his toe ;
> I'll give him a pill—if it don't cure it may kill—
> And draw him a tooth. Come, help in good truth.
> (They pull at a string to which a large tooth is tied.)
> (Exhibiting tooth) I have cured in France, I have cured in Spain ;
> Rise up, Sir Knight ! and don't fight again.
>
> [Enter Beelzebub.]
> Here comes old Beelzebub,
> And on my shoulder I carry a club,
> And in my hand a dripping-pan—
> Don't you think I'm a funny old man ?
>
> [Enter Bighead.]
> In comes I that's not been hit,
> With my great head and little wit,
> My head's so big, my wit so small
> We've done our best to please you all.
> (Rattles money-box.)
>   W.S.

A Day Out – Aged 12

On a fine Sunday morning, quite an adventure for me! I was going with Dad to Swanbourne to meet Granddad who came from Weedon, driving his trotting Cob and a light cart. We had goods to exchange.

For Dad it was an early start- cows to milk, farm jobs to complete and our own transport was our slow carthorse, Prince, and a hay cart. We loaded our cargo in boxes, with a parcel and a sack of corn, which would be my seat on the way. Prince had only one pace, a plod; our journey would take a long time.

On the way past Whaddon Dad showed me the new water tower at Mursley in the distance. We would eventually pass it and then turn right out of the village to Swanbourne where Gramp was waiting by The Swan public house.

We exchanged our goods. Being late summer Gramp had bought boxes of apples, some very sweet, which I sampled as I tended the horses, while they went into the Swan for a refreshing pint. I hope Gramma never found out that Gramp went into a public house – especially on a Sunday!

On our way back, about two miles from home, one of Prince's front shoes became loose. Dad said that he had been aware of the problem and had put new nails in, hoping it would last the day. Going on slowly, we just managed to get home and Dad pulled the shoe off and asked me to take Prince to the blacksmith in the morning to get it shod properly.

Monday morning – off to Stony Stratford I went, leading this large Shire horse with one hand, carrying the horse-shoe in the other thinking myself a very important twelve-year old.

I made my way to Church Street to W. Roberts and Son, speaking to everyone on the way. I wanted to be noticed.

Arriving at the smithy I could already see a horse in there. I tied Prince to the rail on the church side and walked across the road. I was then aware of a commotion at the smithy. I saw Mr. Roberts, he said they would not be long. They were trying to shoe a colt for the first time and it did not want to be shod.

After some time, the man left with a frisky colt and I took Prince inside. Mr. Roberts had a quick look and told me it wouldn't take long, once his son Rupe got back.

I then saw Rupe coming from the back of the Cock hotel, carrying two-quart bottles. He gave one to his Dad who had a swig then had a drink himself and put the other bottle under the bench, behind a sack curtain, in a pail of cold water.

When he put the empty bottle on the windowsill Mr. Robert's said to me, "Cold tea, my boy, nothing like it for quenching the thirst!".

Soon my horse was finished with both front shoes re-fitted. I got home late for dinner, but the job was well done.

It was to be several years before I discovered the place in the Cock yard that dispensed "cold tea", and very good it was too.

Granddad William Goss

The Air Field

Jack Peverill of Whaddon was talking to father about taking a herd of cattle to some grass fields he had rented near the "Air" field at Shenley. I was unaware of this field and did not ask at the time but talked it over with friends the next day. We agreed that there had been more aircraft about, some days three biplanes-occasionally a monoplane - so we decided to investigate.

On Saturday morning, in great secrecy, we set off for Shenley across the fields. We were soon on unfamiliar ground and lost. We climbed a haystack looking for some sight of buildings, but all we could see was a farm in the distance, so we walked on. We then heard the sound of an aircraft, and a biplane came over flying very low, from the direction of Whaddon. We ran after it thinking it was going to land, but it disappeared in the distance.

By now we were getting tired, hungry and a little scared, so we set off back, hopefully towards home. A woman on a horse with a sheepdog rode over to us and I expected trouble, but she was friendly and asked us if we were lost. I said that we were and told the reason for our journey. She smiled and said, "Oh, my dears, you mean the 'Hare' field!"

She told us the best way home.

A Big Bang

We knew two soldiers from Whaddon Camp; they often called at our house. To us children they appeared quite old for soldiers but were always nice. Both were called Joe.

One winter night they came to the house and said they had to get to Stony Stratford but had only got one bike - had we one they could borrow. At the time Dad was down the yard milking and Mum had popped next door for a gossip, so sister Audrey said they could have Dad's bike. This I thought was most unwise, as non-one must touch his only form of transport. But they departed, and we went to bed.

Suddenly in the night a huge explosion shook the house. We rushed downstairs where mother was still working and Dad not yet in. Several people called wanting to know what had happened. A call to the ARP post was unanswered and no siren had been sounded, but the searchlights were active. We saw nothing untoward. After a while, fortified by cocoa and fresh hot water bottles, we returned to bed.

Much later, still awake after the exciting evening, we were aware of loud voices downstairs. Dad was shouting. I crept down the stairs to listen, as it was very unusual for Dad to raise his voice. It appeared he had come home still not knowing what had caused the explosion, went to the shed for his bike, and found it had been stolen.

As Warden, he set off on foot to Stony only to meet two apologetic soldiers, also on foot, having crashed into each other, smashing Dad's bike. They followed him into the house, promising the bike would be repaired but Dad wouldn't calm down. I had never known him so angry since the day he lost his favourite pipe in the muckle (muckheap).

Next morning calm was restored but no news of the Big Bang. In the morning all sorts of rumours and theories were spread around, the most likely being that a plane had crashed near Shenley and blown up. By dinnertime nothing was certain, so I met up with two boys from Fairfield Cottage and we decided to investigate, so off we went in the afternoon, telling no one. Young Billy was not invited but came all the same.

We went along to the Watling Street and on up that road to Two Mile Ash. We saw a man loading wood on a cart, so I asked him if a plane had crashed. I asked did he hear an explosion last night.

"Dunno." he answered, "Maybe I did, maybe I didn't, and we don't have to talk about things". So, we left, wondering how he thought we would have a link with German Intelligence.

I next asked a lady in her garden by a farm the same questions. "Are you from the bottle dump. I don't know you - you're gypsies - go away!" is all she answered.

As we left for home, little Billy started crying. I shouted, "We are from Calverton and my Dad's an important man".

That night, Dad had the news - a lone German plane dropped a large landmine in fields two miles away, damaging many trees, nothing else, probably aiming at the many wireless masts in the fields around us. A lucky escape!

Perhaps they were looking for my "air" field!

The Highwayman - Finding a Gun – 1941

Messing about in our stable one afternoon, I found a gun in a sack under the manger, I recognised it as one belonging to Doug Castle who, with his father Reg and dog Rags, shot rabbits on Saturdays in the winter.

The gun was a small .3 shot. No cartridges were available in the war, but I thought it would impress my friends. It did. One wanted to buy it, but I told them I was planning a hold-up - I would stop a car and take all their money.

My bragging was soon to get me into trouble. Two brothers called me a coward so, in a moment of false bravado, I said I would stop the next car. For a while the only traffic was on four legs, but then a large car came from the direction of Whaddon. I jumped to my feet, walked into the road and waved the gun. `

The car stopped, and, to my horror, I could see it was a camouflaged car with darkened windows that came through every day to the wireless station at Whaddon Hall. The driver wound down the window – I wanted to say "hands up" but I couldn't speak. I could see in the back seat a huge uniformed man who looked like a General.

I stood there frozen to the spot. My friends had all disappeared. A voice from the back seat bellowed, "Take the gun away from the young fool".

 I let him take it and he asked my name and said he would report me to the police and then they drove off.

Dad arrived. One of the boys who ran away told him what I had done. He was quite cross with me and, knowing nothing of the gun, sent me off home to my mother to phone the police and plead for me. She spoke to Sergeant Rawlings. I heard her say that I had been led on by two older boys who had moved in a year ago and had a bad reputation and had been with me that day.

The Sergeant said he already had the gun. It was a serious business and he would call in the morning to see me. I didn't want to see him as it was only a few weeks earlier that his constable had been to see me regarding smashed windows in Mr. Bates' isolated barn, but I had convinced him of my innocence - I think!!

The next morning, I thought I would go missing but wasn't allowed to leave the house.

It was almost dinnertime when the Sergeant's cream coloured two-seater pulled up outside our house. I ran upstairs while mother made him some tea, then my sister Audrey fetched me to face him.

For a start he really told me off, saying it was against the law being in possession of firearms in wartime. He kept on giving me such a lecture. I felt really guilty and felt I had done something wrong, but, eventually, he softened and said to my Dad,

"Whose side is he on in this war, taking on the British Army?"
Everybody laughed, and he left.

SO ENDED ANOTHER FOOLISH ESCAPADE.

Maurice Goss

The New Goalie

One girl, Barbara Kronberg, asked if she could join us. A recent evacuee to Middle Weald, she had been shunned by the Middle Weald Gang. They had asked her where she was from, thinking she said "Beachampton" they would have nothing to do with her. They hadn't heard of Bucharest. We gave her a sort of one-day trial.

I always skated sitting down as we fooled around. Suddenly Emlyn shouted, "Look out!" as the girl came gliding past me, arms spread out and sliding on one leg. What about that? She can't come again; she's just a show off.

I was soon to change my mind. We had a race to Passenham and let her win. Barbara thanked us for letting her play. I asked her if she played any other sports, she said hockey, cricket and football. Just then we had to hide as the school bus came by.

When it came to football training that spring, every one of us decided that the girl could keep goal, as Bryan was no good. He spent his half time calling the opponents "cheats" because they had only scored eight goals and not the eleven they claimed.

We were a small squad, most of our stars had gone out ferreting, as would I but for team loyalty. We were forced to have W.D. from Middle Weald. I disliked him for having seen "King Kong" at the pictures and continuously bragging about it. I still have not seen it.

It was to be W.D.'s day: he ran through a bewildered defence to score his first ever goal. A pity he hadn't changed ends at half time.

That game would be long remembered for the flurry of kicks leading to Emlyn's shot and score. It was likened to the shot of Pete Mutch who, with his last kick won the cup for Preston against Huddersfield- except Emlyn's was more powerful and collapsed the post. Segments of orange had arrived, so the spectators went to Mrs. Bevington and returned with a long clothes prop for the bar and two pitchforks as posts.

(The 1938 FA Cup was won by Preston North End when George Mutch scored the winning goal via the crossbar during extra time. This was the first FA Cup Final broadcast in full to a national audience of 10,000 television sets.)

Brief Encounter

Mr. How, a widower, moved in to Middle Weald at the beginning of the war. He was one of the first mobile Fish and Chip vendors.

By now retired and in poor health, he drank large amounts of milk with his medication. He would stand in the middle of the road and stop the school bus, asking any of the Goss children to get him some milk in the evening. As the local milk boy, I would then have to take him milk and so I began to spend a lot of time with him; helping in the garden and doing his shopping on Saturdays.

After a year or so, a widow lady moved into a house nearby and began to visit. This very soon led to marriage. I was told I was still to visit and was asked to Sunday tea.

Unfortunately, the marriage did not last, and his wife moved away – life carried on as before. Nothing was heard of his wife who he referred to as "her as was here" until a claim for maintenance arrived which he refused to pay until he was threatened with prison then relented. Thereafter, a trip to E.T. Ray, Solicitors, in Stratford was added to my shopping list. There I crept along a passage, tapped on a window, passed the lady 10/- from Mr. How for his wife, whose whereabouts was for a while unknown.

Then one day Mr. How told me she was a housekeeper in Stony Stratford - he knew the avenue but not the house - could I find out for him which one it was? One of my friends lived in the same avenue and soon found out the number for me. I wished I had not passed this on, as now Mr. How wanted me to take a note to her.

In the note, he requested the return of his copper kettle and his "Home Sweet Home" doormat. She answered the door herself. I gave her the note. She read it, screwed it up and said, "I don't know how he found me, but tell him, until he returns my oil lamp, wicker basket and cushions, the doormat and kettle stay where they are". I never knew the outcome of this little saga. I told Mr. How I could not go to Stratford any more on Saturdays, as I would be working on the farm.

My Rabbit Skin Gloves 1941

Just before Christmas 1941, my sister Audrey became ill, and so I had to take over the milk round. I had often helped so I knew the customers. My bike had only one crate for 12 pints, so I had to use Audrey's - her bike had two large crates for pints and quarts.

This was to be quite an adventure for an eleven-year old whose first problem was getting up early in the morning. The weather was very cold and frosty, and it often snowed, and the roads were frozen. I took half loads as I was out on the road long before "Little Jimmy" the roadman was out putting sand on the hills.

We delivered milk to most of the houses in Middle Weald, some in Lower Weald, but most men worked on farms so had milk as part of their pay in their work, and others fetched milk from Manor Farm. We then had a few customers scattered around Stony Stratford.

My greatest problem was the cold. I had only one pair of woollen gloves knitted by my Mum, but they got wet and my fingers froze. The answer I decided was fur gloves. I had some money from two rabbits I had sold, so off to Wickins the outfitters. I went on Christmas Eve.

The shop was busy, and I was very nervous. I just stood inside the door. Eventually a young man came to my assistance. Off he went, returning with a box containing a pair of gloves. I tried them on - perfect. I was now about to get my first lesson in economics, the price was £1.0.0. I quietly told him I hadn't enough money and how much were the cheapest. He then found some basic gloves lined with rabbit skin for five shillings. Could I take them and pay the other shilling next week?

The proprietor was called and told of the situation. He was very friendly and asked my name and said that he knew my parents well and they were good customers.

After I told him I was a milk boy with cold hands, he took pity on me and I walked out with 4s/Od gloves – so pleased I hardly ever took them off.

Wild Food Enterprise

There were plenty of blackberries to pick from the hedgerows. Once all our needs were met at home, I would take all I could pick to a small sweet shop in Silver Street, run by the Misses Elliott, where I was generously paid in sweets of their choice - never mine. Taking them on Monday on the way to school, I would arrive with pockets full. News soon spread, "Goss 'as got suckers!" I always had many friends on those days.

A great bonus occurred in late autumn one year when a bumper crop of mushrooms appeared. Dad's friend, Reg Castle, came up at dawn, found all he needed, and told we children where they were; so off to Spring Hill where we soon filled our baskets and went home for more. Dad found more in Little Bunker when he turned the cows out, so we went there before dinnertime and had such a surplus, more than we needed. Then I thought of the Miss Elliotts, so off to Stony Stratford with my bike and a large box of choice mushrooms.

One of the sisters who ran the shop was so thrilled she called the other sister to see them and asked whether I could get some more. I said I could and would take them the next day; she gave me some sweets and asked me to Sunday tea.

This got me off matins on Sunday morning; my friend Emlyn said that if I wasn't going to church, he wouldn't go either, so he helped me find another box full of mushrooms which I tied on my bike carrier, went off to the shop and ate a good tea.

One of the sisters (I could never tell them apart) asked if I would like to wait until the next week and have some fireworks for the mushrooms. I had never had any of my own, so I was pleased and shared them with Emlyn. We were not allowed any rockets in case we set fire to the hayricks - as if we would!

My Parents with brothers and sisters

Blackberries and Unexpected Words

After the cowslip heads picked for wine, there were acres of orchids on Spring Hill whose smell and vibrant, various shades of purple fascinated me, but after picking a bunch and realising that they couldn't be sold or eaten, interest waned.

From mid July, when the weather was favourable, some mushrooms would grow, but the best of this bountiful summer was yet to come. Fruit was abundant, especially blackberries: Picking them would keep us busy. There were no boundaries where they grew- only one farmer did not like children.

It was Doug Harper, who had been tolerant of myself and my friend, Emlyn, until a family moved in who he suspected of stealing. We were often with these boys so were not welcome on his land, as I was to find out when collecting firewood from under one of his trees. He came over to me and clipped my ears, so for the moment, I kept off his land.

When the time came for making blackberry jam, all the family went picking with baskets and boxes. These were all filled and large amounts of sugar awaited with the huge cooking pot. Enough was cooked sufficient for the year, going into the pantry store.

When the grocer delivered the sugar, the box was so large the driver could hardly carry it. What a contrast awaited us when rationing began.

One Sunday afternoon, needing more blackberries, I knew a field where there would be plenty. In Harper's Paddock, a long field of ridge and furrow well known as a good blackberry area, I soon filled my box at the bottom of the field when I noticed a sheep on its back in a furrow. This is not unusual at the end of the summer when they get top fat, fall over and soon expire. I knew what had to be done and, with difficulty, rolled it over and back on its feet.

I heard somebody shout, it was Harper. I grabbed my box and ran away.

That evening, when Dad put the cows out into the field, Harper came over to him,

"That boy of yours- I saw him from the garden."

Dad feared the worst.

"I didn't know what he were doing till the ewe were back on her feet. I don't know how he turned her. Saved her life. You're lucky to have him. Good lad."

Dad hurried home to tell all- a compliment for me! The news spread.

Bring out the flags, this didn't happen to me very often!

.

Cricket 1940/41

There was an army camp under canvas in the grounds of and behind Calverton Place in 1940-41.

They held a morning Church Parade, sometimes filling half the church, but more often they marched to Old Wolverton or Whaddon, while those from Whaddon camp would march the four miles to Calverton Church.

One Sunday, Dad told me that there was to be a cricket match at the camp against a visiting army side. I couldn't attend church when cricket was being played so went to the field behind Calverton Place, where hundreds of soldiers were, like me, having a Sunday off church. The field had been mown and a good pitch prepared.

I remember nothing of the game itself, but I did remember it must have been played mostly by officers because they wore a wonderful array of caps from pre-war Public Schools and Clubs.

Catching Rabbits - My Pocket Money

Every spare weekend and holiday from school was spent in pursuit of rabbits. I always took older boys with me, as I didn't like putting my arm down the rabbit holes. The two boys who usually came with me were already poachers. I took my dog and our sheepdog, and as we walked past Fairfield Farm, looked out for George Cowley's multi-coloured collie - a powerful dog and a good rabbiter.

When out with me one day he caught and killed a fox and ate much of it. George didn't like his dog to hunt but the dog loved to come. We usually made for two gorse fields left to go wild and infested with rabbits. There were few warrens- most of the rabbits lived above ground, with single holes for shelter, which made their capture easier. We ran the dogs' round until they went into a hole. The dogs would bark and scratch until we found them, and the rest was easy.

We usually caught two or three or more good clean rabbits, which fetched 2/-d each and were in demand. One boy two years older than me brought his ferrets and was expert at skinning. He said that he would skin the four we had that day and we would get 2/6d for them.

I took one to Mrs. Knight who was pleased to have it oven-ready, and another to the Rectory where they would have two a week if possible. Miss Taylor, the housekeeper was also pleased with her skinless rabbit at 2/6d, but a few days later I saw Miss Taylor again who asked me not to skin any more as she had been reprimanded by the Rector for her extravagance, as he sold the skins himself for 9d.

The Hortons and Cigarettes

The farmhouse at Dairy Farm became vacant. The War Office took it for one of their men at the Wireless Station at Whaddon.

Mr. and Mrs. Horton and son Alan, aged 15, moved in and I became friends with Alan who told me his father was in the Secret Service. I guess he was connected to Bletchley Park but, at the time, we knew nothing about this side of the war.

Mrs. Horton began to call at our house each morning as she cycled to Stratford to buy cigarettes. They were very scarce at the time. She often called on the way home, reporting the length of the queues, the brands she had found and how many. She often had to go to Wolverton if she had not found enough, and also got mother to put 20 Players on her weekly grocery order.

At the time I couldn't think what she did with them all and we lost touch when we left Calverton. Now I think she was probably selling them on at a profit to the workers at the Wireless Station.

MARKET SQUARE AND WESLEY'S TREE.

Young Farmers' Club at Bletchley Park

Bletchley Young Farmers' Club meetings were held on Saturday mornings at the Park, rent free, by kind permission of Lady Leon, then owner of the house.

Sister Audrey and I had joined. The great thrill for me was that we would be conveyed by motorcar driven by another member, Miss Jean Holland. I was so keen that we had walked to the White House in Oak Lane before the car was prepared. I sat on the grass and watched as the handle was turned. Eventually, after a few tries the engine fired and jumping up quickly, we were off, me in the back.

The front screen was clear, but the rear windows were yellow Perspex cracked like cobwebs denying me any light or view.

Off we went to Bletchley, up the grand drive and parked at the front door. This was the first of many trips in the old car, but I never knew the name of the blacksmith who made it.

"Follow me." said Jean as we entered the mansion, along into a room with an open door. Inside a few people and some posh furniture. Up got a man with a bunch of keys in his hand, which I noticed he never put down. "I am Mr. Brant, the County Secretary, I will be taking the meetings." Chairs were set out in a cleared space. Brant opened the meeting.

"Livestock and husbandry will be our subject. In conjunction with this subject, we will form a calf club. Each member will adopt a calf, feed it, groom it and train it to the halter and present it at the County Show where awards will be given."

"I shall leave." I whispered to Audrey.

"You will not." came the reply.

So be it.

The meetings became too much like school. I watched Mr. Brant unconsciously juggle his keys.

The weeks and months passed. The Show bought us no awards.

Then, some months later, all changed. Mr. Brant met us at the front door. We were told that the room was no longer available. A major refurbishment was taking place, the family would be moving back to the Manor. The deception had begun.

We were offered the glass conservatory into which we squeezed for several weeks. Then it was decided to disband the club for the duration of the war.

Farewell to Bletchley and to Mr. Brant, he could put away his keys and move to a cushy job with the Ministry of Agriculture. We were to meet again many times in the future.

The Motorbike

Emlyn, Brenda and I went to see the gypsies in Oakhill Lane. They told us of an accident on the Watling Street close by, involving a lorry and a motorbike. So off we went to investigate. We were surprised to see the motorbike still lying there and hardly damaged.

As there was no one around, we decided to take it home. No easy task. For at about 11 years of age, I was no taller than the handlebars. Nevertheless, we pushed it the mile back to Calverton between us and hid it in the hedge in Donkey's Close.

In the afternoon the local policeman called at our house. Emlyn had gone missing and I could not remember where I had been that morning, so he interviewed Brenda. She did nothing but cry all the time, despite him telling her that he had three little girls at home and they did not cry when they saw him.

The day was saved when Tom Goodger, who found the bike when fetching in the cows for milking came and told the constable "It 'ud be they gypsies what pinched it."

My First Paid Work 1940

Doug Harper farmed Fairfield Farm until 1938 when Mr. Cowley moved there from Common Farm. Mr. Harper made cheese in one of his buildings. The smell was so strong we couldn't smell the piggery next door.

Mrs. Harper sometimes put a bag of cakes or biscuits on the roadside gatepost with a note saying, "Please take one". My friend Emlyn and I only took one at a time, but suddenly they were all gone.

It was Mr. Harper who gave me my first chance to work with a horse. I knew the horse well. He was small and black, called Nigger. He was a veteran of the First World War with an army tattoo on his flank. Though mostly retired, he was used to turn the gear that worked an elevator: tedious but not hard work.

I was watching the hay being off-loaded and Nigger stopped several times. Mr. Harper on the stack asked if I would get a small stick and persuade the horse to keep going round and round the drive shaft. This I did and enjoyed it for the rest of the day.

I went home with my first wages - 2d. (Two old pence-less than 1p)

Old Time Graffiti - and a New Puppy

Cycling home from school one Friday afternoon, I stopped by The Shoulder of Mutton public house to look at a steam engine in Mr. Fountain's walled paddock. This was formerly the Manor rabbit warren. I spent some time looking and climbing on it and then returned to my bike. I then noticed the nice clean, red brick wall adjoining Mr. Gerrards' house.

Having two sticks of chalk, acquired from school, I thought of several items of news I would make public. (I have no idea what they were). Being the half-wit I was, I put my name to it and went home.

Next morning - a Saturday - after a phone call from Mr. Gerrard, saw me off to Lower Weald with bucket and mop on my bike to clean the offending chalk with water from a spring nearby. Although it did not take long, no one had seen me the previous afternoon, but this morning everyone I didn't want to see me came by as I cleaned, adding to my embarrassment.

Mrs. Gerrard came and approved her clean wall, gave me a cup of tea, and showed me three· puppies aged nine weeks. I played with them a while, and then she asked if I would like one. "Yes please, this one", I said, picking one up.

They were mongrels she wanted a home for. I took the puppy home in the bucket with a towel tied over the top, and Mrs. Gerrard asked me to take the pup back regularly, so she could watch its progress, something she would live to regret as I often took her at her word!

I kept the dog "Penny" for four years moving her to Weston with our sheep dog. Unfortunately, both dogs were poisoned down on the allotments at Weston Underwood.

Haymaking 1940

I next helped haymaking in the field called Little Bunker, taking time off from school.

I worked the horse and rake, dragging the hay into rows, while Mum and Dad heaped it up into haycocks. I could not do it very well as the hay rake needed the right arm and leg to work it, meaning that both reins were held in the left hand to guide a horse with its own ideas of the direction he was going.

By four o'clock Mum went home, returning with an enamel can full of tea and some jam sandwiches, which we ate under the oak tree.

The following Sunday, I went with horse and cart to Whaddon to fetch a hay sweep, a wooded type sledge which pushed the haycocks to the stack in the field, much easier than loading on to the cart first.

It was a quiet road that should have been empty, but I met a large army convoy. For each wide lorry I had to pull on to the verge, but I pulled the rein too hard, sending the wrong signal to the horse, which turned round in the road and started heading home again; taking much persuading to turn back to Whaddon. There was much shouting and advice from the lorry drivers as I held up the war effort learning to drive a horse on the road.

Haymaking with Tom Goodger

Tom Goodger had a smallholding opposite our farm - sometimes I helped him with his haymaking. He also had a full-time worker always known as Johnny.

Like most small farmers, Mr. Goodger had no wagon, just a pair of two-wheel farm carts that were converted for hay by extensions at the front over the horse and at the rear, these gate-like fittings we called copsies. They were a frame extension with four corner posts with ropes fixed from back to front to hold the load secure.

Making hay on his farm in good weather was organised but leisurely. Each day enough grass was mowed for two cartloads, then it lay for a day and after the next day's cut was done, it was turned and rowed up.

This is when I joined them, jumping on the cart and enjoying the gentle plod of the horse as we went to the hayfield. The cart then went between two rows so that two men could pitch the hay from opposite sides. I as the load binder levelled the load with a fork and walked round and round to tread down the fluffy hay that came up to my middle.

After one load I would climb down by the ropes and we would go on with the second cart. This time I lay on top of the load of sweet- smelling hay for the ride back to the farm.

Here Mrs. Goodger, a strange woman who wore a khaki smock and Wellingtons, and little else, made a great meal for us of scones, jam, cream and good strong tea.

After this we emptied the loads onto the stack and I collected tuppence, leaving them to milk their cows until haymaking again the next day.

Harvest 1942 (Age 13)

When harvest began, I went to help Mr. Cowley on his farm at Lower Weald. My job was to lead one of the wagons to the field to be loaded with sheaves.

I usually built the load, roped it with help from the men, climbed down via the rope, and then back to the farm, being careful through narrow gateways. The hardest part was leading the horse and wagon alongside the elevator. I had never done this before and the man unloading wanted me closer while the men on the stack were telling me to get wider or I would crash into the elevator.

I found this all very frightening but managed somehow. Work progressed gently in the week, but at weekends soldiers with farm experience were released to help. We had three with us; so another horse and cart were used. The soldiers enjoyed the work as they avoided the route march and church parade on Sunday.

We were surprised at the number of men who came on Sunday offering to work but realised many other farms did not work on the Sabbath.

The next week was very hot and one teatime I was asked to take two horses to the pond to drink. They went into the deep water taking me with them. One stepped on my foot, pushing it into the soft mud. I escaped with a big bruise, but I was allowed to ride on the horse for the rest of the week.

Some of my days Threshing

After a day's threshing on Mr. King's smallholding, I went on to Monty Woolard's at Shenley Hill Farm.

He had a tractor-driven thresher called a peg drum, brand new from Canada. These all-steel machines had a conveyor only five feet from the ground. The sheaves were thrown on without cutting the strings, and this made it very fast. Five men instead of over ten on the traditional thresher were all that were needed. The straw and chaff were blown into huge heaps but was of no use and so was burnt.

Mr. Woolard was the farmer who paid me more than the basic pay, saying I'd worked like a man and would be paid as one - 30 shillings for one week – but like all my earnings, it went into my Savings Bank.

Father asked me to go to Mr. Luckett Senior's Brick Kiln Farm to thresh. He used a small tractor to drive the machine, not as I preferred, a steam engine, but quite adequate. We threshed here for four days. When we lined up for our pay, Mr. Luckett walked past me saying, "I will see your father". I was disappointed, but I think we owed for a sack of seed corn.

Some of the last days threshing that year were at Mr. Luckett's Stacey Farm, Wolverton - now the museum. A long five-bay barn could only be worked from the end, so the sheaves had to be thrown the length of the barn. Brother Basil, myself and two land girls fed the box. It was freezing cold and very hard work with only one break.

After two days two more girls arrived so I left and returned to school in time to leave.

I next reported to Mr. Bennet, Rectory Farm, Lower Weald, for two weeks threshing.

"How much do they pay you then boy?" were his first words to me.
"Five bob a day, Sir, 'cause I never stop work", I said.

"You'll be carrying the water for the engine", he said, so collecting the buckets and a yoke and a plough line for a rope, he showed me the well in the orchard. This was a fair walk from the rick yard. I tied a bucket to the rope and threw it down the well.

It was difficult to get out because it caught on the sides and spilt the water. "She'll drink a lot of water", said Mr. Starsmore, the engine owner, "so you'll not hang about". I did not. It was a rush to feed the thirsty monster.

We had a hard frost later that week and the rope dropped in the well and got thick with ice and was very cold to pull up. However, by Saturday morning of the first week I had the tank of the engine full for the first time, only to hear the engine driver say,

"She'll freeze tomorrow. I'll let the water out". I watched hours of work run down the ditch.

The next week we threshed barley, the price of which had risen from £4 a sack to £14, a fortune at that time, but it did nothing for Bennett's generosity, for when it came to payday he said,

"I've looked up your pay, at 14 you only get 4/- a day". And that is what he gave me.

Good job he did not know I was only 13!!

A threshing gang at work

Whitehouse Farm

I spent a day at Whitehouse Farm helping thresh a stack of wheat for George Holland (known as Rat Face owing to his unappealing moustache curled at the end) It was a good place to work: tea was brought out twice in a day.

In wartime, it was compulsory that every corn stack being threshed be surrounded with wire netting to prevent the escape of any rats, and there were regular visits from the police checking, and heavy fines for any offence.

Mr. Holland did not put wire round his stacks, as it was soon apparent, there were many rats in the stack.

This day, I was on the stack digging out the sheaves with old Tom and a very large lady I had not seen before - I found out she lived in a bus on another farm with a son and many daughters as her husband was in jail at the time -but on this day I feared for the ladder when she climbed to the top of the stack.

She wore lots of bright red lipstick and had very red cheeks, looking like a post-box. The men were very rude about her at lunch time when she went off to the orchard. Old Tom said that she had legs like hovel posts and a rear like a carthorse.

By the time the roof was off the stack rats began to run about trying to escape. We killed many of them and the farmer, with a big stick, tried to get those running for the hedge.

When we got near the end there were so many the farmer, panicking, ran to the barn, emerging with a double-barrelled shotgun and a canvas bag of cartridges. He immediately opened fire and shot many rats, but, after a while, he climbed on the stack shooting, putting us all in danger. The engine man told him to "Get off that bloody rick" and, waving his arms about, shouted that he would stop the machine. George got off and soon, to our relief, he ran out of ammunition, and we were able to finish our day's work.

Threshing at Shenley Dens 1941

Shenley Dens, a neighbouring farm on the road to Whaddon but in the Parish of Shenley, was the home to the Phillips family. Ted Philips, a large and very strong man, had, I believe, come over with the Australian Army in the 1914-18 War, and stayed in this country. He came to the Dens in the late 1930s.

Like many farms in these years, The Dens had suffered in the depression with several fields rough grazing for the sheep. The fields were covered with huge ant banks and molehills and grew lots of thistles and wild flowers, especially early purple orchids and later orchids. We played in these fields and its pond from a very young age.

My first visit to the farm itself was for a day threshing a stack of beans. I worked on the stack digging out the sheaves with a fork. An old man called Joe, then passed them to the thresher. Mr. Philllips carried the full sacks to the barn.

The beans were few, the thistles abundant. The wind blew the thistledown like snow all day. The prickly thistles got in all our clothing, my hatless head of hair had a grey look, and it was quite a miserable day.

Suddenly in the afternoon, great excitement, the engine man opened the door to the fire to stoke up and a flame from the fire set light to the thistledown that covered the engine. We all rushed to help beat out the flames with thick corn sacks, and water from the engine's tank made it safe, a great relief to all, except to me who had secretly hoped for something more spectacular.

When we finished, I was asked to the house for tea. We were joined by a neighbour who asked me if I would go to his farm the next day with his thresher. Being a glutton for punishment I said ,"Oh, yes!"

I did not get paid by Mr. Phillips as he would come to help us thresh wheat two weeks later in return. On that day he worked on the rick himself almost single-handed, being a very hard worker.

At dinnertime, mother cooked a meal for him, but he got on his bike and disappeared to "The Mutton". At two o'clock he was still missing. After a while Dad sent me to tell him we couldn't manage without him. I timidly opened the pub door. He stood at the bar, smiled, and came at once.

Mr. Cox

When Mr. Cowley left Common Farm in Calverton, Mr. Cox took over and Dad arranged for me to go and help before he told me.

The Sunday before, I went with two Rainbow brothers with a dog, ferrets, and catapult to catch rabbits.

We saw a hare sitting in a field and two of us walked on as the hare watched. Ken, who had stopped behind, took the hare with a single pebble, a well rehearsed plan.

Shortly after we were caught by Mr. Cox, on his land and he was very cross. He asked Buster Rainbow, the eldest, his name and he cheekily replied "William Shakespeare and his brother" for which he was hit by Mr. Cox with his stick. I was so scared I told him who I was and that I would be working for him in the morning. After this he was fine but told me to avoid older boys for they would get me into trouble.

He let us off - we retrieved the hidden hare - and I had a pleasant week working on his farm.

Reluctant Artist

During my brief return to school, I attended my only ever Art lesson by our master, Mr. Cheeseman (Cheddar) - our subject to paint being a copy of a coloured conker leaf gathered from one of the trees outside the school, the best paintings to be displayed in the hall.

Paintings finished, we handed them in to the teacher. Some I could see were very good - mine, even for a first attempt, was a mess.

The class was told that next we would paint our first portrait. The thought filled me with horror. I must get out of it somehow - but how?

After my week of apprehension, we had a talk about the subject and it was announced that I was to be the model! Sigh of relief!

This was great, sitting on a stool in front of the class, the centre of attraction, long unkempt hair, polo necked jumper up to my chin, grubby knees. I was an obvious choice for the master.

He sat at his desk reading while various attempts were made to capture this image, he added that they would have a lesson next week to complete. He only interrupted once when telling the class to stop giggling and me to stop pulling faces. At the end of the lesson he told me to make sure I attended next week for the completion.

That night I made a BIG mistake. I told my mother my portrait was being painted next week, but not that it had already begun.

Off to Barber Meakins, a friend who caught rabbits on our farm and didn't charge for the haircut - a sharp cut that left most of my hair on the floor. I was almost unrecognisable.

On the day of the Art lesson I was sent to school in a white shirt and tie, causing much ridicule and mirth.

Mr. Cheeseman said nothing until the Art lesson when he told the class to ignore the new Goss and continue with the old. The outcome was mixed, some, especially the girls made a good image of such a challenge, but my classmates all took the chance to greatly exaggerate my large ears on show after the severe haircut. I could only hope these caricatures were never seen outside the class.

That was my last Art class and almost the end of my school days. The lure and opportunities to work with the steam thresher were too great, despite the pleading and protests from mother.

Trouble Brewing

My parents had been talking about my absence from school for months now. Dad said he would have to find me work soon after Christmas; Mum said Dad had got to stop recommending me to the neighbours saying, "I'll send Maurice round to sort that out"

A change would have to be made: I was out of control.

One night, Dad came in, riddled the fire, wound the old grandfather clock and stepped on to the stairs and shouted up,

"Are you awake?"

No reply. I thought to myself it might be time for a listen. I only heard him say, "He must be told." so I thought they must be talking about me, but they were speaking more quietly now, so I had to wait until the next morning. Then I learnt that Mr. Cheeseman - known to us boys as "Old Cheddar" - had apparently been at the meeting the previous evening. They had had something to discuss- me!

The schoolmaster had described me to Dad as "a wild colt that was in need of a strong tether", what could that mean? Good or bad? There seemed to be no way out, school it must be. After my lecture from Dad, I strolled into class as if nothing had happened; neither a hero nor villain was I. The Master was looking up from the register.

"Good Morning, Sir."

"Ah, Goss, nice to have you amongst us."

"Thank you, Sir. I am afraid I have forgotten my homework."

"I'm sure you will be afraid, Goss, you will have plenty from now on, you have a lot to catch up on. You are way behind the rest of the class, now, get to your place."

Why can't I keep my bloody mouth shut? Never mind, the last six months hadn't been totally wasted.

It had turned very cold. The classroom windows were covered with thick ice and the fish tank had ice on it. The frost never really thawed all day. Central heating? There was none, just one coal fire to heat the whole of the classroom. Nothing to be done now but count the days till Easter.

The next Monday the bombshell dropped: the outside lavatories were frozen solid and we would all have to be sent home. I was distraught! A coach was rescheduled to take village children home at midday. We could not possibly go home at that time of day, so I called a meeting of the Upper Weald Gang. We would all go skating, non-members excluded.

Leaving Calverton

Despite my long periods of absence from school, in my last year neither the Headmaster nor the teacher ever asked for an explanation. Attendance Officer, Mr. Batchelor ignored me. They knew all attempts to educate me had failed.

However, I had the audacity to attend on the last day of term to say farewell. I no longer had a desk! Mr. Cheeseman, with a wry smile, said, "Goss, didn't you leave last year?"

The day passed pleasantly- I was fourteen and about to make an impression on the world!

The war at this time was making a great impact on the smallholdings of Upper Weald. Whaddon Hall, the secret wireless station, was spreading its receiving masts across the fields, almost to the houses of the village.

Then came the bombshell; a visit from the men of the War Office.

"We are commandeering your farmland, you can keep the house, but we will take all of your land- you have ten days to clear it."

My dad asked, "What for? Is it something to do with Whaddon?

"Nothing to do with Whaddon, we need it for a firing range."

Dad was in a state of shock. He had for some time been hoping for a bigger farm, now we had no farm at all.

I never knew if any other land was involved or what weapons would be fired- it was apt that one field was called 'Butts Piece'. As the name suggests, it would have been used for training back in the time when village archers practiced their skills.

We as a family were stunned. Mostly we were concerned for the livestock. Dad's precious cows, what would become of them? And us?

Suddenly, from despair to great excitement! Dad spoke to a cattle dealer friend who could maybe help. A farmer he knew may be moving from his farm and would consider a tenant.

Out into the World

At last, what schooling I was to have, I'd had. My sentence at school had been served. What should I do: farm work, join the army or run away to Australia? While I was making my plans, so too was my mother. She told Audrey I was to be sent away. In fact, I was to go to work on a farm of her sister at Marsh Gibbon, thirty miles away. I know I had been a disappointment to her, but this seemed a bit drastic.

Mabel, a widow of moderate means, with four adult children, two of whom were at war, had been a house keeper for Robert Parker, a bachelor aged near seventy years old. He was a wealthy landowner and farmer who had several small local farms. They had recently married. She was my mum's older sister. Perhaps this explains my presence there. I was thinking 'might I do well there and get rich someday?'

I had never met them or knew what they looked like.
But Saturday next I would find out.

Part Two: Marsh Gibbon
Buckinghamshire 1942

Exile in Aylesbury

The next Saturday my case was packed and loaded with me on the Red Midland bus bound for Aylesbury and into the unknown. My instructions were to find 'Boots' shop and upstairs in the lending library, I would find Auntie Mabel.

I never did find 'Boots'.

I asked a man for the cattle market, "Straight on and follow your nose." Dad had told me Bob Parker would be the poorest looking man, but he would be buying the most cattle. I went off to market to look. Seeing a man wearing his oldest clothes, old-fashioned gaiters, boots well oiled to preserve them as long as possible and an ancient cap on his head, buying cattle round the ring, haggling over the price and state of some of the animals, I instinctively knew my search was over.

My First Year at Marsh Gibbon   March 1942

We arrived at Marsh Gibbon about 4 o'clock to start work immediately. Bob did not drive the car himself, his car driver was Mr Hadland who ran a small butchers-shop in Green Lane. He sold one type of meat at a time, depending on the weather and what animals were available: first it would be a lamb, and then when that was sold, he would have a pig, then a beast.

We lived at Vine Farm in the village. I slept in the attic, which I reached from a ladder on the landing; the room had one small window too high to see out of, a small bed surrounded by boxes containing twenty years of receipts, old farming papers and election addresses, several from George Bower, Lord Denham's father. These I noticed as being from Weston Underwood where my family moved to in my absence.

The land farmed at Marsh Gibbon by Bob, other than Vine Farm, which only had a few paddocks, was Heat Farm where the cows were milked, a farm opposite on the turnpike road, two fields in Blackthorn Road, three in Bicester Road and three meadows at Twyford. He also had farms at Bierton and at Ford. These farms were sold for £35,000, a huge sum of money in those days. He also rented at Creslow. For all this land he had one workman who he paid, named Jack Leach, and he left three weeks after my arrival. I then became the complete workforce at fourteen years old.

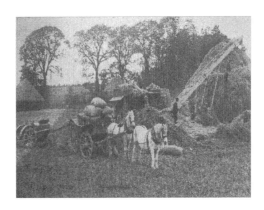

The Working Day: Never take your boots off till the sun sets

Our day began at 5.30am when Mr Woods the carrier, who also had a smallholding, called at the farmhouse for a cup of tea; this he drank while his cows wandered from his fields in Bicester Road to the dairy opposite The Greyhound pub. Each morning began for me with feeding the pigs over the road at Vine Farm. The feed was a concoction consisting of barley meal, potatoes, and carcasses of sheep and calves cooked in an old copper. The sheep were collected from the surrounding area; all the wool was pulled off the stinking bodies first and later hidden in in the fleeces at shearing time. I always thought it would have been nice to have eaten our breakfast of bacon and eggs before handling that foul stew!

After breakfast at about 6.30am we drove the two miles down Green Lane to Heat Farm to milk 16 cows. We travelled in the cob and float (pony and cart). There was one shippen (cowshed) for six cows, the rest were tethered in hovels.

Bob would leave for the market about 10am. If we sent stock, Bob would ride in the cattle lorry, otherwise he was taken by car. I would attend to the sheep, which usually meant catching the lambs with maggots, pouring disinfectant on the wound and rubbing the maggots out with my fingers. (I have never been tempted to keep sheep over the last forty years!).

After finishing on this farm and other odd fields, I drove a few miles to Twyford. Here at Twyford over sixty cattle grazed the river meadows; these cattle were often out in neighbouring fields and would take hours to sort out. Odd ones swam the river and then the farmer on the other side would try to buy them cheaply, knowing we had to bring them back several miles along the road.

Sometimes I had dinner back at the farmhouse, but if Bob was back from the market early, he would bring my dinner down the field wrapped in a tea towel. After this I spent my afternoon digging years of muck from the cattle sheds. It was about six feet deep and almost impossible to untangle. My working day at Marsh Farm was from light to dark through the summer with no days off. "Never take your boots off till the sun sets. (not even on a Sunday) There is always something to do" were his favourite words. After milking I would take the cows to graze the roadside a mile off. Bob said it was the best grass because if was free.

In the afternoons we loaded two wagons and conscripted two men from his cottages to help unload in the evening. They were not pleased as they had both cycled to Calverton brickyard and back and worked a twelve-hour shift each day.

World war 11 poster

The Man from the Ministry

We had at this time a visit from a Mr Brant of the Agricultural Office. In the war all farms were graded according to how well they were farmed. AB and C. (If graded C you were supervised), and Mr Parker's farm was supervised. Mr Brant could see we would never finish such a big hay crop without help, so he sent a gang of men from the labour pool to help the next week.

On Monday the men arrived at Heat Farm and looked what they were, the dregs of the pool: two conches (conscientious objectors) and three foreign interns. They were unfriendly, not keen on work, and one was terrified of horses. "I shan't pay them," said uncle. He was told they would be replaced when another gang became available, but this did not happen, so he finished them after three weeks. After a month haymaking was finished at Heat Farm and moved over to the Grange to gather two good fields of hay.

There's always something to do

Apart from these tasks of feeding stock, milking cows, which was of course done by hand in those days, the shearing of the sheep was my first big job. A small farmer from the next village did the shearing and rolled the fleeces while I turned the handle of the shearing machine and caught the sheep. He was on piecework, I was on overwork.

Around this time Bob would be off to large cattle sales, buying truckloads of cattle, some to arrive at Poundon station the following morning. They were walked through the village to Heat Farm, many being sold on the way to local farmers, keen buyers of his stock.

Apart from being a cattle dealer of some considerable merit, Bob was best known over many miles as a castrator of horses. I went with him on some of these trips, one time going to London to attend to horses at 4 guineas a time (£4.20p.) He was locally known as Bobby Cutter.

I had little time to mix with the local boys who I found to be mostly unfriendly and even hostile. One I did befriend worked on the next farm at Mr Hunters; he was unfortunately killed when the horse he was leading bolted when stung by a wasp.

Marsh Gibbon had about eighteen farmers at the time. Only eight farmed more than 150 acres. There were not many tractors about: most of the work was done by horses. Most farmers had fields in the hay meadows along Turnpike Road, and on fine summer evenings you would see many groups of haymakers within half a mile of each other loading the wagons with pitchforks.

When we started haymaking, we began by mowing grass in Blackthorn Road. One evening, it was about 6 o'clock by the time I had been shown what to do, I was left to get on with it; Bob did not tell me whether he was coming back or when I should stop, so I carried on working until dark. As we had double British Summer Time then, it was very late when I rode the horses back through the village. People came to their bedroom windows thinking someone's horses had got out.

A Bungling Burglar

In April, soon after my arrival in Marsh Gibbon, Uncle Bob and I called on a Mr Parker the builder to ask him to erect a gate and a roadside fence.

However, Mr Parker was in the Forces, while the business was being run by his wife and one worker. They were very busy. But we were told of an Irishman who was looking for work, so we saw him, and he came to work the next morning.

His name was Graham, and I worked with him for three days and how interesting it was- he was on remand, charged with theft.

He had spent time in prison for burglary. He had broken into a lonely farmhouse while the owners were away. He used their wheelbarrow to carry away his booty, drinking at least one bottle of whiskey on his way home. As he had left wheel marks all the way across the field to his house, and the barrow, with some items still inside, was left in his front garden; it was not very long before he was caught.

More Ministry Meddling

Most of the land at Marsh was ploughed pasture in the spring of 1942 but ploughing orders were imposed on two fields on Heat Farm and were promptly ignored. However, in June, the Ministry of Agriculture, not a body to be ignored, sent an Oliver Tractor with orders to plough the fields. Meeting an unrepentant Robert Parker in the gateway with a shotgun was enough to send him back to Buckingham.

On the second visit with government officers in attendance Bob's mind was not altered.

"Why", asked one "do you not retire at your age; why go on working?"

"I go on working for you lazy b*****s who won't" was his short reply.

However, after going to Court and paying a large fine, the fields were ploughed and a good crop of black oats was grown.

Word of Home.

The farmhouse was home to three London families either on holiday or victims of the blitz. Uncle asked them if they would help with the war effort by helping with the hay. At first, they were very keen, the next day we had more workers than pitchforks. A few soon got blisters and not many came the next day, and none at all after they discovered that uncle did not intend to pay them.

The hay was ready so back to the labour pool. We were next sent three girls who were Polish Jews. They were hardworking and quiet and spoke good English. I had to build my first stack with them and we got on quite well. By the second day, the girls began to talk and ask me about the village. I said I did not know much about it, as I was a stranger. I then told them I came from Calverton but my family had since moved to Woodlands Farm, Weston Underwood. To my amazement they told me a great deal about my new home; I had never seen it.

They had spent the whole of last harvest at Woodlands. They told me all about it, and the wonderful wheat crops it grew. This persuaded me I wanted to go home for harvest when the hay was done. I left for Woodlands where I met the same three girls again a year and a half later when they came threshing.

Woodlands Farm Cottages

Return Visit 1943

When I returned for the summer of 1943, the village was much busier; gangs of Italian Prisoners of War wandered around the village in the evenings, sometimes trying to buy beer from the local pub. They had some money but were not allowed to go into the pub themselves but would hang about outside waiting for a friendly local to buy it for them. I was a local, but I had no money so were of mutual benefit. Also, there were troops from the nearby camps and they would cram into The Greyhound every night and their singing could be heard all over the village.

I bought a bike and had the occasional Sunday off; sometimes I would bike home to Weston, a round trip of about 70 miles. This year things were a little better on the farm, there was a tractor to mow the grass for hay. A gang of girls from East Europe worked well in the hay fields. They spoke perfect English and were very keen to get to Israel as soon as the war was over. Mr Heritage, and others who lived in Bob's cottages, were pressganged to work in the evenings, already having worked a twelve-hour shift in the local brickworks.

A bombed-out firm of Rawlings and Hunter had moved into Marsh and had taken over the two downstairs rooms of the farmhouse, using the telephone all day to 'phone worldwide. Little did they know that the safe under the table on which they worked was full of gold sovereigns. I never did find the key!

Sunday was the only day we could use the living room and, if I was not working, I watched the world go by from that window. Mr Lambourno, with his bible under his arm, was off to chapel and, in the other direction, Mr Heritage the hay-tier was on his way to the public house dead on opening time, were part of the village life going on outside.

When haymaking had finished, I was once again on my own most of the day. The Slaymakere family who had lived in Heat Farm had left and the days seemed long and lonely at this isolated farm. So, in August I decided to go home to Weston and help with the harvest there. The day I left, taking my depleted wages with me, my aunt insisted I buy some of her eldest son's cast-offs and a trouser press-all the things she thought I could not possibly do without. I trudged off to Poundon station carrying two very heavy suitcases. This time I had to walk, unlike my arrival when I came by car.

Dad had heard that there were Italian Prisoners of War allocated to Woodlands. He had wondered if they would be locked to a ball and chain, wear arrow suits or have bars at the windows, like in films. He was, on arrival, horrified that the POWs had borrowed guns and were up the woods, shooting rabbits. He got on well with the POWs at Woodlands- they were northerners and would not associate with the southerners on the other farms. They borrowed bikes to visit the Two Brewers in Olney, one of them courting a barmaid there. They had been farmers until the fascists made them join the army, now they were farming again they didn't want to cause trouble. Dad gained a good knowledge of Italian swearwords from them.

Oak Tree named after William Cowper the local poet

Part Three: A Weston Underwood Miscellany

The Farms of Weston Underwood

Pheasant's Nest

Charlie Goodman farmed Pheasant's Nest – both his sons were in the Army. He employed Ted Adams (Dennis's father) and Bert Adams who had been conscripted from the Manor Gardens. He also had a Jewish land girl, Betty Cohen, who lodged with Phyllis Foster.

Charlie was a mullacker – a local description of an unhurried, unenterprising man. He was quite happy when his old machines broke down and he could go into his workshop to repair it.

He grew good crops, but much was wasted. We were twice directed by the War Agriculture Officer to help with his harvest. We cleared Spring Bank in a day but when we got to Dysons, the sheaves of wheat lay on the ground where the binder had left them weeks before and they had grown into the ground. We carted them off somehow and took them home to the stack. Ted Adams was a very capable worker, able to do all farm work but spent too much time round a small dairy herd. One of Goodman's sons back in England obtained 14 days Special Leave to help with the harvest but spent all this time on an old motorbike and thought that the land girls were much more interesting than the harvest he was supposed to be saving.

On a cold windy day, the following March, I joined a motley crew to thresh at Pheasant's Nest. Three Land Army girls, Goodman's staff and myself, were hindered by old Bill B. and Jack E, both from Olney, who were unemployable in peacetime, but farms had to employ whoever was available. They both came to work in their long Home Guard overcoats down to their boots. Jack was given the dirtiest job, clearing the chaff and caving from under the threshing box. Because the sheaves had so much dirt in them through laying so long in the field, this dirt became dust when it dried and it was impossible to see the person next to you. Also, the straw was so rotten it broke up, much of it finishing up under the machine with the husks and the chaff.

It was obvious that Jack would never keep up with the output, which he had to carry in a cane skip on his back, through the barns and into the hovels around the yards. When the machine was blocking up, Jack took an oil pot as he walked through the barn and squirted some on a belt so that it came off. No one saw him do through the dust. The farmer and Ted dried out the belt and searched for the oil leak, while old Jack cleared the backlog, whilst we all smoked our Woodbines and pipes.

It was an enjoyable farm to work on. I arrived about 8 am. Ted would be raking out the dampened firebox to get up steam and we would start about 9 am. All other farms started at 7 am in pitch darkness. One day it rained all day, so we sat in the barn. Only Ted Adams went off to find a job. The rest of us listened to Goodman's endless stories – many aimed to embarrass the land girls, but the young girls from Lancashire who had all worked together in a tile factory in Leigh before joining the W.L.A. were well able to survive in a man's world and gave a good as they got.

I took the sacks of corn off the machine, weighed them off at two and a quarter hundredweight and carried them into the barn. The wheat was awful and contaminated with soil. The oats in another stack were very good. The sacks weighed only one and half hundredweight, which I carried up the steps into the granary, which is now a house.

I enjoyed working at Charlie Goodman's; not least for the meal they insisted I shared with them every night.

The Goodmans left the area after the war for a farm in Sussex, taking all their livestock and machinery on a special train from Olney.

Babbs came to Home Farm in Olney in the 1940s. He had been a smallholder at Thornborough when his wife came into money. After a couple of years, he bought Pheasant's Nest at Weston amalgamating the two farms – about 500 acres.

He was a poor farmer, employing an army of unskilled young men from Olney. Nothing ever happened on the farm before nine o'clock in the morning and very little afterwards. Babbs was often seen around the farm with his huge bull mastiff dog, the largest dog I have ever seen.

Despite his being a large man with two hands on his rope, the dog used to pull him round the farm at a trot. At times the dog ran loose, terrifying anyone who went near his farm. Several people I knew climbed trees when they saw it approaching and the local poachers knew it was a farm to avoid. Babbs was a large, amiable man, a compulsive braggart whose exaggerated stories changed at each telling; comparing his latest tales was a favourite pastime in local pubs and markets.

When he had to stock his large farm, he went to Scotland and bought hundreds of half-breed mountain sheep. They came to Olney station on the train. These sheep then became the talk of the district – the poor fencing on the farm, plus the fact that the sheep had been accustomed to grazing half of Sutherland. They did the same in North Bucks, and parts of Northants.

They soon arrived at Eakley Leyes and a farm in Yardley Hastings, village gardens, and allotments were ravaged. They climbed up on the park wall, ran along the wall into the Manor Gardens where the efforts of the three gardeners were wiped out overnight.

There was a large stack of Lucerne hay by Chestnut Walk and as the weather got colder the sheep helped themselves, pulling it from the bottom. After a few weeks they had eaten so far under the stack that only their rear ends could be seen. Fearing the hay would eventually fall and bury them; he offered us the hay, which we bought.

Elder brother and myself arrived with two tractors and trailers and hay knife to collect. It. About thirty sheep were feeding but ran off as we arrived, apart from four. Pulling them away we found them dead and they had been for some time.

Although they were a hardy breed, many more died that winter. Babbs later sold the farm to Mr. Marler and went off to a pig farm in Norfolk.

"Peasant's Nest."

Shearing at Cowper's Oak Farm 1943

Jack Birch did not look like a farmer, which he wasn't!
He looked like an insurance man – which he was! A
tall, sandy-haired, bespectacled man, he moved in with
his wife, Maggie, and two children to Cowper's Oak
Farm in September 1942, from Milton Malsor, in
Northamptonshire. There he had a small-holding, in
addition to being with The Eagle Star Insurance Co.
which he then left to be a full-time farmer. He moved
his possessions on a wagon pulled by his horse, his
Tamworth pigs by pony and float, and walked his
livestock along the country roads.

By the spring of 1943 he had a flock of about 40 sheep,
mixed breeds. The day before Whitsun weekend he
came over and asked if we would shear his sheep for
him, as he did not know how. Dad said that he would
come on the following Monday and I would help him –
the fact that it was Bank Holiday Monday mattered not!
Jack said he would get the sheep in all ready for us, if

he could find them. I knew it was going to be one of those days. A lovely hot Monday morning found us walking to Cowper's Oak, as there were trees across the ridings in the wood. I carried the shearing machine on my shoulders. This was a tubular metal contraption, three feet high on three legs, a gearbox on top, with a handle to drive it. A shaft with an elbow in it drove the clippers.

I caught the sheep, after helping to get them in and turned the handle. Father sheared the sheep. Mr Birch had his usual bad back, so he rolled the fleeces.

Mid-morning a sheep kicked the machine and broke it – the first time I had known one of these machines to break. It was decided that we should borrow a similar machine from Mr. Graves at Weston Underwood and I was sent to fetch it. I ran through the woods to the farm, then cycled to Weston.

"Course you can have it," said Austin Graves, "we shan't want it today – it's a holiday!" So, fitting the contraption across my shoulders, steering one-handed looking like a trick cyclist, I rode back to the farm.

Then, for the second time in the day, I carried a machine up the hill and through the wood- at least one and a half miles – exhausted. I found the others in the house, the teapot now cold. "Let's get on with" they said – no tea for me!

Eventually Birch said that he would shear a sheep, but he couldn't keep it still – it kicked incessantly, shredding the fleece to fragments. When it did stop kicking, he finished it off only to find the sheep was dead.

A month after shearing his sheep, Jack Birch asked us to stack a field of hay which was already in the swathe in the field near his road. So, on Saturday morning we loaded a hay sweep on a trailer and drove all round the road through Olney (approximately six miles), the wood still being blocked by felling at the time.

We fitted the hay sweep on the front of the tractor and Basil drove the tractor up the rows, pushing huge piles of hay up to the stack. Jack Birch and I pitched the hay on to the rick (no elevator). Father built the rick helped by one of the forestry girls who lodged at Biggin Lodge – at other times felling timber in Kilwick. The other girl had a horse and rake and dragged the hay into rows. We finished at 9 o'clock. Basil drove the tractor back through Olney. We had supper at Cowper's Oak farm. Then Jack Birch fetched out his chequebook to settle up. Father charged £4 10s for the haymaking and the shearing. I remember wishing he had charged him £5 for I had no wages and had no money at the time.

In the spring of 1944, the land girls finished felling 400 oaks in Kilwick, left the lodgings at Cowper's Oak and were replaced by Italian prisoners. Despite this abundance of labour his harvest was still unfinished mid-September and, as usual, we went to help out.

I went all weekend carrying and stacking the wheat to ricks. We worked until dark on Saturday, got finished at 5pm on Sunday. We had a meal – harvest supper in the evening. The Italians walked to Olney R.C. Church – down through Kilwick, joined the two Italians from Hungary Hall and, from there, to Olney.

Our two Italians would not go with them because those four came from Southern Italy and our two from the north. Ours said all who lived south of Rome were lazy villains and thieves. Mrs Birch became concerned when they had not returned by 9 o'clock – then curfew time – but thought they were probably at Hungary Hall farm.

As I was about to leave, having had a good meal and having drunk the modest contents of his cellar, the prisoners returned with sacks and bags of apples and pears, the produce of most of the orchards in West Street. Mrs Birch was at first alarmed but was soon sorting out the ones most likely to keep until Christmas.

Jack attempted to grow a field of mangolds in the field under Kilwick and grew the best crop of weeds I've ever seen in my life – planted the seed with our Suffolk drill – the seed grew but so did the weeds, especially redshank whose seedlings are similar to mangolds. So similar it made hoeing a nightmare.

Jack, whose eyesight was very poor, overcame this by having a hoe with a handle one foot long to be near the crop. He went down the crop on two feet and a hand and looked a strange sight from the wood gate where we watched him one day – looking very similar to a kangaroo with a smock on! He always wore a khaki smock.
Jack told me so fast did the weeds grow that, if he had a long dinnertime, he couldn't see where he had got to.

After spending some weeks on this hopeless project, the problem was solved when his sheep kept getting in and he decided to leave them to eat what they could find.

Jack's Tamworth Pigs

Ginger Tamworths are the nearest breed of pig to the wild boar and Jack's were almost the real thing. They lived as a communal herd, all sizes and ages together, roaming in the woods, lazing in muddy ponds and racing off in all directions when disturbed. At night the only way to get them inside a shed was to entice them with food and slam the door fast.

Jack asked if I knew anyone who would kill two fat pigs for him, this being in 1943 when the Black Market was at its height. I knew just the man – Jim Adams, a single man of about thirty and a trained butcher home on leave. Jim was a great character – a drinker and ladies' man, and always keen to earn a few bob.

I took him to the farm one Sunday morning, not telling him there were two land girls living there. Jim killed the pigs and spent the rest of his leave there at the farm.

Higgins Lodge Farm

Ted and Amos were bachelor brothers who lived at Weston Lodge, otherwise known as Higgins Lodge. They were builders from Cosgrove. Their father, Amos Senior, was a farmer at Cosgrove. He took the farm in 1939 to keep his sons out of the army, farmers not being liable to call-up. They left as soon as the war ended.

Theirs was a Spartan life – they never went out. They had an old brown three-wheeled van. The only visitors were their parents who came by pony and trap every Thursday – mother cleaned the house and did some cooking, while father looked at the farm and told them what to do as they had little knowledge of farming. They were hard workers and quite inventive, having a wind-driven generator that could be driven off a motorcycle engine when there was no wind for lighting the house. Weston Lodge buildings were two small cottages that had in the past been homes to large local families.

When Amos arrived, a hole in the wall converted them into a small farmhouse. After the war (Leatham from Ravenstone) rented the farm and an old couple called Fountain, who had farmed at Warrington until they went broke, moved in and did a little work for their keep. In 1947, in the deep snow of a severe winter, his wife died, and it was two days before he could get down to Ravenstone to let anyone know.

We took urgent telephone messages for the Amoses. One day Eddie, my brother knocked on the door and window, but they had the wireless on and could not hear him. After he had been there some minutes, the back door suddenly opened, and Tom threw the tealeaves all over him, not knowing that he was there.

John Digby: Greenways

We called John Digby "the midnight farmer". His farmhouse was Greenways, comprising of the meadow Patches and Pans, sold from Hungary Hall, Hill Field, which is part of Weston Park, Dudley Charity field that was ploughed up in 1943. In all there were about 120 acres. He had recently left Higgins Lodge and before that had been landlord of The Wheatsheaf at Ravenstone. Throughout the war he employed no one, relying on neighbours and contractors to do his work. He himself never seemed to do anything until everyone else had finished and would then be seen with his hurricane lamp seeing to his stock well into the night. He built himself a cowshed at the bottom of his garden, but that brought the wrath of the District Council down on him and he was never allowed to use it. I think they feared that the drainage would affect the wells lower in that field that supplied the whole area with water.

Hill Field grew a crop of Holdfast wheat that was the talk of the area. Some said it was as much as one and three-quarter tons to the acre; ploughed by two tractors hired from the War Executive, one driven by Ned Walters, an experienced tractor driver and the other by a novice land girl, who Ned was teaching to drive. These tractors had a blind at the front to warm them up. Ed noticed that the tractor the land girl was driving was boiling so stopped his tractor, went over to the other tractor, which he did not stop, walking backwards in front of the tractor, winding down the blind, fell and was crushed by the tractor.

The girl stopped the tractor on top of him and fled. Digby heard the scream but would not move the tractor, so cycled to Stewart's farm, borrowed Tom Bacon, tractor driver, to recover the body of the unfortunate man who died through his own folly.

Austin Graves: Church and Park Farms

Austin Graves was a pleasant easy-going man, typical farmer of that time who unfortunately did not live long enough for me to get to know well. He was good to work for, never expecting too much from his workers and he never got too much.

Charlie Whiting was a dedicated shepherd who kept his flock mostly in the park, which remained pasture until the late 1940s when a part of it was ploughed.

I used to see him each morning when I took the milk down, carefully going through his sheep and he regularly walked the park wall to see no stones were becoming dislodged. Vic Adams, Len's father, was the tractor driver and also helped with the milking. He worked well but complained profusely of his old Titan tractor, which, in hot weather, boiled all day, needing a water cart in the field and his old Oliver plough, which he never quite mastered.

Dennis Adams was the herdsman and milking man. He treated the stock as his own and his whole life was centred around his cows.

Ted Adams Senior was the horseman and approaching retirement, as were George Shouler and Freddie

Clifton. The later would never have found work had it not been for the generosity of the Graves family.

These older ones found the walk to the mangold field to hoe so exhausting that little stamina was left for the job in hand. I helped with the threshing at Woolwich barn following a week at Stewarts. They shared the same equipment. We threshed inside the barn and outside, but the days seemed very long from 7am – 5pm. We never left there all day or had a cup of tea.

Hungary Hall Farm 1942

I arrived in Weston during August 1942, four months after the rest of the family, having been at Marsh Gibbon.

Bill Reynolds became tenant of Hungary Hall in September 1942. Hungary Hall farm had been bought by Mr. Litchfield before the war for £1,500. It was then 230 acres. He sold off Patches and Puns Meadow and later Dickin's Spinney or Bluebell Wood; so, the farm was about 200 acres. Babbs from Pheasants Nest kept pigs in the adjoining barn and ran them in the wood.

The harvest was ready and two Italian prisoners had moved in. After our harvest was finished and the ploughing done, I, being the youngest at work, was at the end of the pecking order when jobs were allocated, so did the work others rejected. I was then told I could go to Hungary Hall for the winter to help Bill Reynolds who was on his own, so I willingly went and stayed two winters there. The first time I saw Bill Reynolds was a Sunday morning when he came down the railway with his sow, which had escaped.

The first task at Hungary Hall was to clear out the farmhouse with the help of brother Eddie, who was off school, and our horse and cart. We emptied the back room of old wireless batteries, gin bottles, tobacco tins and other necessities of life, left behind by the late tenant, Stan Chennells and his wife who had moved to Olney. In the front room we found most of the newspapers of recent years. In the papers we read newsy scandals of which we were not aware, being newcomers to the area. It took us so long to find the following day's papers to find the relevant stories that the job took some time!

The previous tenants, the Chennells, had lost their only child a few years before and one of the upstairs rooms was decorated out as s nursery and was in spotless condition, with the cot and toys still as they had been.

When the house was emptied and cleaned up, I went to Olney with the horse and cart to collect building materials for Morgans who were to repair and decorate the farmhouse.

The rest of the farm was all scrub – tall thorn bushes, ash trees and gorse. Some parts of the farm hadn't been visited by anyone for years. Mr. Chennells told me that rabbits and pheasants had always paid his rent.

In that winter of 1942-43, these clear fields were ploughed and planted with flax, a flax mill having been built in Billing nearby. The flax was used mostly for webbing on army uniforms. This was the first time I had ploughed with an iron-wheeled tractor and two-furrowed plough.

The crop was planted in March and was harvested with a purpose-built machine from the War Ministry, which pulled the flax then tied the bundles like a binder. In the early summer of 1943, a pair of large steam engines, owned by Savage of Riseley, arrived firstly to pull trees and bushes with wire ropes to clear more fields for ploughing.

Four men accompanied the steam engines, living in the week in a large wooden-wheeled caravan. In it were a cooker, table, chairs and bedding. Each engine had its own driver. The other two men shared the cooking and manual Work. They worked very long days, from about 5.30 in the morning – although I was never that early to see! – Until 8.30 at night and 2pm on Saturdays when they would bike back to Riseley.

For the first week, the engines filled with water from the two farm ponds, driving to the ponds to fill up several times a day – sucking up water with a hose. After about a week of pulling the bushes the ponds were dry and the well empty, so with our iron wheeled tractor, a connected horse drawn water cart, and with great enthusiasm, I set off on Monday morning for Danes Close pond to carry water for these two thirsty monsters. I had never had such a responsible job before – excitement was short-lived! The small rotary pump on top of the tank took over two hours to fill the tank, lifting the water up 12 feet from the pond.

The weather was very hot and dry, especially that day. By 4pm the tank half-full on my third load, I heard three long blasts of the whistle of one of the engines which meant the water was low, so after some frantic pumping and further blasts on the whistle, I rushed off down the field with a nearly full tank, in top gear – the iron-wheeled cart finding every hole in the track. An ill-fitting wooden lid had the hard- won water cascading all over me when I went through the dried-up brook at the bottom of Danes Close. When I got to the engine, he stuck his pipe in the tank and within a minute it was empty – so off again I went! Filling an engine at 8pm, the driver thankfully said that that would for the day but wait – the other driver asked me to fetch some more so that he could start in the morning. He knew he would want to start before I was up, so I had to comply.

The method used to clear the scrub was to put a wire cable round a group of bushes and gently draw the cable which was attached to a drum under the engine (like a huge cotton reel) but it left huge tangled heaps that had to be sorted and burnt by hand with great difficulty. The farmer himself did most of this work. Once started, these fires smouldered for several days (despite the blackout).

Bill stopped only occasionally for food and sleep. He started off the week clean and shaved but, by the following weekend, his well-grown beard, like the top of his hat, was thick with wood ash. On Saturday afternoons, the workmen returned to Riseley and with Bill away for the weekend, calm returned until the Monday.

After the first week of carting water, my early starts got later so permission was gained for the steam engines to fill themselves each morning from a dewpond in nearby Dysons or Pheasants Nest. This gave me time to go to Olney station with our horse and cart to fetch a load of steam coal; the engines' appetite for coal being as great as their thirst for water. I was scared to take the cartload of coal down the steep hill, carts having no brakes. I feared the horse would lose its footing. So, I came round by Woodlands, called in for breakfast, took my time hoping someone else would fill the "bloody" water cart.

The deep digging tines of the cultivator tore up large strips of earth all tangled with roots, but exposing fine black soil showing the promise of the good crops it was soon to grow. The first time the cultivator was drawn across the field at a depth of about one foot, it was quite comfortable for the man sitting on top of the machine on his iron seat who did the steering. But when it was done in the opposite direction to shift any portions not moved the first time, the ground was so rough that the machine tossed around like a boat at sea. The two men had to change over every two hours instead of once a day.

After some weeks the engines left. We picked up all the roots we could then ploughed the land. I had hoped to do the ploughing but the iron front wheels on the lumpy ground made steering too difficult for me. At times it took the wheel out of my hands bending fingers and wrists. So, Bill himself took over. He sat on the tractor for hours on end, creeping along in bottom gear. He stopped coming out with us in the evenings and was often at work when we came home at night.

The land was twice ploughed then laid fallow. There were good seedbeds. Then a drill was hired from the Government store at Newport Pagnell. The wheat was soon planted and grew well.

With the harvest came the problems. The crops were good but there were few workers available – most land girls were now in regular permanent work on farms so the only people available were from the Government labour pool. They consisted of conscientious objectors, foreign aliens and Italian prisoners of war. Bill liked none of them. He said the conchies won't fight, Italians won't work and the Europeans he couldn't understand were probably spies.

There were continuous rows and frequent sackings. The new Australian-made Sunshine binder refused to tie a third of the sheaves – a fault non-one could rectify. This made the standing up of the shocks slow and frustrating – so many sheaves having to be tied by hand.

Whatever your FRONT LINE JOB

This is your SECOND LINE JOB

LEND A HAND ON THE LAND

The weather turned wet and caused considerable delay but soon men from the village and around the area came to help at weekends and at nights. Some came in the evening after finishing work on their own farms. Such was the fervour of the war effort at the time and farmers in general were then held in high esteem.

The first harvest was threshed by neighbour Charlie Goodman's vintage steam threshing machine, with a very unsafe threshing box with many holes on the top which, when covered with straw, became a hazard for the unwary. A very old elevator that did not fold for transport was stowed behind it. It was this that blocked the railway for an hour when the engine failed to pull its load up the incline by the Fir Wood. Flagmen on the railway held up the trains while Ted and Bert Adams, the driver and mate, used a wire rope winched to the trees to clear the line in the process uprooting several of our trees.

The wheat yields were good. All three downstairs rooms in the farmhouse were filled with four bushels (21/4 cwt.) sacks of wheat, carried on our backs from the thresher in the rick yard. Two of the Italian POW who helped with the threshing remained to live and work on the farm for the rest of the war and I returned home to work. The only stock on Hungary Hall Farm then was one sow and her offspring, until in the autumn of 1942 when Bill had gathered together some ewes of mature years and varied breeds. At the Ram Fair at Northampton, he bought a find black-faced Oxford ram.

On the following Sunday, Bill being away I fed the pig and went to the pond field which still had a fair covering of bushes, to check the sheep. Seeing them at the top of the field I sent my sheepdog, Tarzan, to bring them down the field to me.

To my horror, as the sheep came towards me, the new ram just keeled over. When I got up to it was stone dead. I did not tell anyone about it in case I was blamed for running the sheep. I took the coward's way out and left it for Bill to find on Monday. Fortunately, Bill got most of the money back from the vendor.

The grazing of the fields from the Firwood to Kilwick was let to Jack Peveril. I did the shepherding. Jack was a dealer who bought anything in market that was cheap and might "grow into money".

Apart from the cattle of all sorts, there was a mare which proved to be in foal and gave birth unattended, but when the foal was about six weeks old (this again on a Sunday) I found it dead under the elm trees by the farm. I phoned the owner who told me to bury it.

On Sunday afternoon I took my spade and dug the grave for the unfortunate animal. Whether it was lack of judgment or the optimism of a 15- year old, or just the hard ground, but when I pushed the young foal into the hole, it over-flowed and its feet were sticking out of the top. I couldn't get it out again, so I fetched the milk pony from the farm and a rope, pulled it out, and got back digging.

Weston Underwood High Street

Pastures New Spring 1945

In the spring of that year we took grass grazing at Bozeat, in Northamptonshire on a five-year lease. We walked the first sixteen cattle there on a Sunday morning.

By the time we got to Olney was after 10 o'clock in the morning so that we should miss the milking herds that used the High Street daily. Brother Basil and father went in front in the car. Myself and two Italian prisoners, dressed in their uniform with bright coloured patches sewn into them, were on our cycles behind or by the side of the cattle to block off any side roads.

All went well until we got down to the High Street where several roads meet near The Castle Public House.

Some cows were in front, Dad in the road, Jim by West Street, Joe in Yardley Road, and a fair number of spectators joining in the fun.

Suddenly one beast broke free, heading up towards Moores Hill. Joe biked after it and two other men moved over to prevent the others following. Joe caught up with the runaway, hitting it on the nose with his stick, the only way to turn a beast. Once this was done, Joe got off his bike and walked the cow back down the hill towards the others.

Suddenly a woman with her own stick stepped off the pavement beating Joe with it shouting, "You hit that cow and I'll beat you" It was quite a vicious assault so Joe managed to make his escape on his bike again. He dare not defend himself for fear of getting into trouble. We decided she must have had a reason to dislike Italians, but we all had a good laugh about it – especially Joe himself.

Things settled down after this and we went on through Warrington, which was a winding road round several cottages at that time, where the herd managed to get into a cottage garden. Were we pleased to find no one was living there at the time!

Several hours later, we were thankful to get them all into the new field of grass and shut the gate.

Weston Underwood High Street

New Pony and Float

We had two horses when we moved to Weston and soon realised, we needed a pony and float to take the milk churns to the village each morning to catch the lorry due to the carthorses being too slow.

We bought a chestnut cob and float for £35 but it wasn't much faster. The cob was supposed to be about eight years old but was probably eighteen. As you can't really tell a horse's age until it is seven, to dealers like Billy Marston all horses were eight. The poor thing was broken-winded and could only trot about twenty yards at a time.

I took the milk down in the mornings; three or four churns and collected four loaves straight from the baker's oven. Beyond this the horse refused to go, presenting problems if it needed to go to the blacksmith's at Ravenstone. Every morning Charlie Covington gave me a cigarette for bringing our post and the post to John Ruffets in the Keeper's Cottage. John at this time could no longer walk – he was a huge man, over 20 stone, and he sat all day in his chair overlooking the Park. Sometimes he would keep me, telling his stories of his job and details of all known poachers. If I was more than a few minutes late the horse would plod on without me, threading its way past the L.B.C. lorries that were bringing ammunition to the huts on both sides of the road right up to the farm. Where the road was too narrow gaps were made in the hedge and the ammunition huts were in the edge of the fields.

I would then walk up the lane, talking to the soldiers and civilian lorry drivers whose lorries were commandeered from the brickworks to ferry the ammunition from Turvey station to the huts in every road and lane in the area. When I got home the horse would be waiting to be turned out in the field, his day's work done. About twice a year he would miss our turn and go right up to Higgins Lodge.

The Scapegoats: VJ Night

"The best firework display I have ever seen"

My father said of Weston Underwood's celebrations for VJ night. After six long years, the war was finally over; victory meant change was coming about. Servicemen and women would be returning from all over the world to take up life where they left off or try to. Mechanisation had developed quickly because of the labour shortages; would there be work on the farms for those returning to the workforce? Would there be more food, clothing and fuel available? What would the post war world be like? There was a lot of uncertainty. But for now, the village would celebrate in style.

Army ammunition sheds up Wood Lane were plundered of anything that would make a bright light or a loud noise, a whole range of flares and explosives.

It was truly a village occasion, everyone in the street, from the cottager to the magistrate, out to celebrate victory in a memorable riot of colour, sound and excitement. A competition ensued, flares aimed down the street and through the Knobs, (the "bed knobs" of the stone gateway in the High Street- narrower then.) The village had never seen anything like it!

In the cold light of morning however, someone had to take responsibility for theft and destruction of Government property. This fell upon eight village youths who rode off on bicycles in convoy to Newport Pagnell Magistrate Court. The list of names was mostly farm workers or tenant farmers who never saw the inside of a court in the rest of their lives. How much blame lay with this group my Dad was never clear about. The unnamed fifteen-year old I believe still lives in the village. Anyway, the youths were fined 2/6d each, a collection in the Cowper's Oak covering their expenses.

Below is the article in which the Bucks Standard reported on the events in the magistrates' courts. There seems to be some sympathy from the civilians involved, though the army representative does not share their tolerance. Perhaps it was the sheer scale of the loss of army equipment involved in the celebrations!

VICTORY REVELS AT WESTON UNDERWOOD

RAID ON ROADSIDE MUNITION HUTS

VILLAGE YOUNG MEN CHARGED WITH LARCENY OF EXPLOSIVES

Seven young men residents of Weston Underwood, with a boy of 15, appeared before the Newport Pagnell magistrates on Wednesday charged with alleged larceny of explosives-thunder flashes,distress signals, cracker blank, signal light and sound signal rockets- from ammunition shelters in the village. The explosives were the property of the War Office, and during the hearing of the case it transpired that the offences complained of took place on the night when the people of Weston Underwood were celebrating victory over the Japanese and the end of the war.

Seven of the accused young men - one was in Air Force uniform- were

114

Keith David Pratt, Sidney
George Lord Parkins,
Victor Stanley Adams,
Maurice Goss, Arthur John
Hughes, William Charles
Reynolds and Denis Albert
Adams.

All of them were defended
by Mr. Sidney Smith,
solicitor, Stony
Stratford, and pleaded
guilty.

Inspector W Merry for the
police said that the
prosecution appreciated
that these offences were
committed as a result of
enthusiastic VJ
celebrations, but at the
same time both the
military and the police
were anxious that people
should not do themselves
bodily harm by
interfering with
ammunition placed in huts
at the roadside, and
unfortunately might be
there for so time to
come. That was quite
apart from the value of
the articles concerned.
The full value of the
ammunition interfered
with and missing from the
shelters was quite
considerable.
Fortunately, the

defendants did not meet with any serious injury, but during the course of such celebrations some people had been seriously injured. That did not concern him, but he mentioned it to emphasise the danger to persons unacquainted with these various types of weapons in interfering with them without knowing how they should be handled.

Major J C Fowler, officer in charge of No 1 area ASD, said in Wood Lane, Weston Underwood, there were a number of shelters containing various kinds of explosives. Some of these shelters had been interfered with, and as a result he made a check and found a quantity of ammunition missing- altogether 2,153 thunder flashes, valued at 8 1/2d each, 1,130 cracker blanks valued at £1/9/0 per hundred 23 cartridges, single light and sound value £3/11/0 per hundred, 1,611 signal distress Mark 3, value £9 per 100 and 12 signal rockets. The total value of the missing property was £372/14/10 halfpenny.

It was not alleged that the defendants stole that amount.

Cross-examined by Mr. Smith, witness said the shelters were examined on August 16th, and the loss reported to him the following day. He could quite definitely say that all the things mentioned were removed between the 16th and the 17th. The whole of the boxes were not checked, but the holders were so secured that it would be impossible not to see if things had been taken. The dumps on the roadside have been there three years, but he had no knowledge that they had not previously been interfered with. He was not aware that on the 16th a line of army lorries appeared beside the dumps.

Did you know that soldiers had these things loaded on lorries and were handing them out to children? - I am aware of such a case and the personnel concerned have been dealt with.

Witness did not know that soldiers after

distributing these things
had left boxes with
ammunition lying about.
Mr. Smith said he was
going to suggest that any
interference with the
dumps was caused by
soldiers not by the
villagers.
Answering further
questions by the
defending solicitor,
witness said he did not
know that these things
were being fired all
round Buckingham on VJ
night. He further
suggested that this would
never have happened but
for the fact that a few
soldiers were getting
hold of these things and
not only using them
themselves but handing
them out to children.

Witness: I have no
information to suggest
that any of our personnel
handled quantities in
such a way.
Is it true that the
contents of these dumps
are now going to be
destroyed?-That at the
moment is a matter that
has not been settled.
There are no orders
giving such instructions.

Do you know that they are
now drilling holes in the
boxes so that they can
sink them in the ocean? –
I am not aware of it and
am quite prepared to say
it is not so.
Is it true that the
militia themselves have
fired these things off in
local displays? - That
is so.

What is good for the
military is not good for
the civilian? -Not
necessarily.

By Inspector Merry: the
displays given by the
military were by consent
of the War Office and
were let off by competent
persons. If let off by
persons who knew nothing
about them, they might be
most dangerous.

P.S. James Turney (Olney)
said at 1 am on Friday,
August 17th he visited
Weston Underwood and in
the vicinity of the
(arch?) found 44 empty
distress signal cases.
On the following Saturday
he found ammunition in
great disorder in Weston
Underwood Park. The

sergeant gave details of
an interview he had with
one of the defendants
who, he alleged, told him
that, with other
inhabitants of the
village, he took part in
VJ celebrations and let
off thunder flashes and
distress signals which
they got from shelters in
Wood Lane. Witness added
that his inquiries in
this case occupied seven
days.

Cross-examined, the
sergeant said that on
this particular night
Weston Underwood and
Lavendon were the only
places where these things
were being let off.
P.C.Cook (Olney) also
gave evidence and spoke
of interviews he had with
defendants and read
statements made by them
in which it was alleged
they admitted taking
ammunition which they
took into the Park where
people were letting off
fireworks. One of the
lads denied taking any of
the "fireworks".

This concluded the case
for the prosecution, and
Mr. Smith addressed the

Bench on behalf of the eight defendants, all of whom were natives of Weston Underwood and had served their country well, either in the Cadets, the Air Force, the Home Guard or the N.F.S. They had been perfectly frank when the police came along and admitted taking part in the celebrations. He was instructed that a Justice of the Peace was there, enjoying the fireworks. The atmosphere on that particular day was such that everybody wanted to celebrate and the whole village wanted to. The ammunition boxes were lying about in the Park and people suffering from some form of hysteria would be tempted on such an occasion to go and help themselves, never thinking that they were committing the serious and grave offence of Larceny. He referred to the good characters borne by the defendants and suggested that justice would be done by binding the lads over….
(Unreadable line)…had really no criminal intent.

They dismissed the case under the Probation of Offenders Act and said that each defendant would have to pay 2/6d costs.

The magistrates were Lucas Salmons, (chairman), H B Baldwin and Mrs. Good.

From the "Bucks Standard", September 29th 1945

A Weston Character: "Poacher" Turns Gamekeeper

A local character, Tommy Fox, resided in Weston Underwood prior to my father's arrival but his various exploits were still told by the older villagers who had known him. John Ruffitt, who was the estate's gamekeeper, told the majority of these stories. Dad said Tommy still had relatives locally, so I have changed the name to protect the reputation of the family!

Thomas Henry Fox was born in Lavendon, came to Weston Underwood in the early 1900s, and married Mary, the daughter of a Weston Taylor. They lived in a small cottage in Pevers Lane. Tommy was a farm worker on the Estate, a likeable man with many friends. But Tommy was a compulsive petty thief and like many others, a poacher.

He would never steal from poor folk but would steal for them. Although he had but a small garden there were many large ones in the village, so he would have vegetables or a rabbit for anyone in need. He never charged the very poor, no questions asked, no stories told. Tommy also repaired cycles in the long shed in his garden.

In 1920 things changed, much of the Estate was sold and the farms split up. Many men lost their jobs, including Tommy, with little chance of work as preference was given to ex-servicemen. Poaching and bike repairs and bike dealing became his main income.

Over the next few months and years he would visit different towns where people were gathered, but mostly Northampton. It soon became obvious to his friends that he wasn't buying all these bikes, but he had money and he was generous in the pub and they all had good bikes.

Many years later he told his friends only once was he scared. He had been asked by Billy, the Estate Foreman, if he could find him a strong bike. He was a large man, not popular with the men. He didn't visit the Cowper's Oak, so he didn't know the bike might be dodgy. When going into Northampton one day, Tommy saw a sturdy bike by a gate at the allotments. There was no one near so he parked his old bike by the gate, picked his time, grabbed the better bike and made for home.

Feeling pleased with himself and his acquired bike, he stopped at the pub in Hackleton for a pint. When refreshed, he stood admiring his bike in the pub yard when he noticed a plaque on the saddlebag that read "Northamptonshire Constabulary"

Another important point in Tommy's chequered life came after a visit from keeper John Ruffett who called on him unexpectedly one day.

"I know what you're up to Tommy, you're not buying bikes at the market, you're stealing them. You will go to prison for a long time. It's my job to uphold the law, I must report you."

Tommy was stunned. After the Keeper left, Mary came home and he told her of the Keeper's visit and the trouble he was in; confessing to selling stolen bikes but not saying who had stolen them. Mary was shocked and very angry, "What will people say?"

Tommy left the house.

Mary decided to visit Mrs. Ruffett, a friend with whom she had once worked. When she arrived at Keeper's Cottage, John was at home so she spoke with them both. The outcome was that nothing would be done at the moment, but Tommy would not be told. He was to have time to reflect upon what he had done, Tommy had been a friend to many but a fool to himself.

It seems that John gave Tommy a job as Assistant Game Keeper. He must have been impressed by Tommy's turning over a new leaf, and the enthusiasm with which he took up his new job.

Vermin were strictly controlled on Weston shoot. Anything that might harm a pheasant or eat an egg was killed, especially a fox, although foxes were reared on the Estate for the huntsmen. On the day of the meet, Fred Foster would take a fox from the pen at Laundry Cottage to the woods for the hounds to find.

From April pheasant's eggs were collected and broody hens were brought from the farms and cottages, good prices were paid. Each hen would sit on twenty or more eggs.

John spent most of his time at Weston looking after the chicks. Tommy spent most of his time in the wood getting ready for the arrival of the pheasant pullets. The Keeper's hut on the edge of the wood by Danes Close was a fine refuge on shooting days and for the Keeper's everyday use. It was well built; it had twin oak panel walls and sawdust between for insulation. It had a large brick fireplace and a slate roof. A barrel of beer was kept behind the door, as the boss also owned a brewery.

This, he said to the Keeper, was the best time of his life-and he was getting paid for it!

The Weather 1947

Heavy snow, intense cold, record floods, excessive heat, prolonged drought – that was 1947.

The year started wet until 20 January, when we had a heavy snowstorm. It then snowed most days until the end of March when heavy rain and thawing snow gave the worst floods every known.

Our farm road was totally blocked from 23 January by huge snowdrifts as daily falls were blown off the fields by freezing northeast winds that blew the snow between the ammunition huts that were by all the roadsides – some drifts almost to the top of telegraph poles.

On the Saturday, Mr. Steward gathered his men and tractors and made a track across the park where much of the snow had blown off, to meet the family in our lane with a box of groceries, which had been delivered, and left in Laundry Cottage. We had dug through many times in the week or ten days with snow blowing back.

The ten days' milk we had by us were then taken down to the village on the tractor, the empty ones had been dragged up from the village with ropes, having been left in Weston by the milk lorry from Buckingham. The full churns were so frozen the milk had pushed the lids off the churns – a tin bath also full of milk was brought into the house to thaw.

The following Monday most non-essential workers were stood off by their employers – usual practice in bad weather, and they were then taken on by the Council to clear the roads of snow. Some major roads were cleared with army bulldozers, but the roads round here were left to the humble shovel.

In these seven weeks nationally six million sheep and 30,000 cattle perished. Our waste pipes froze underground, and we had to drive the cattle to ponds and smash the ice with sledgehammers for the thirsty cows to drink. Our cattle cake ran out and we had a delivery into the village where it was stored in Laundry Cottage at Grange Farm until Mr. Stewart and men helped us get it home.

Early April brought heavy rain and with the thaw came some of the worst floods ever known.

It was May before any fieldwork was done and then there was a drought for the rest of the summer, giving the poorest harvest I ever saw – hardly enough to support the thousands of rabbits that had survived the worst weather this century.

All our harvest went into two stacks where other years there had been thirteen stacks.

Just a Hole in a Field

In the corner of a field at the bottom of the Fir wood, close to the railway embankment, was a deep hole with a red brick lining that always intrigued me.

I first saw it in the late months of 1942 when I was loaned out to the new tenant, Mr. Bill Reynolds of Hungary Hall Farm, to clear out the farmhouse for him to move into.

What fun we had with horse and cart and young brother Eddie who was off school. We soon had a load of old newspapers, and every farm magazine the previous tenants had taken in their tenancy despite the lean farming years. They had lived well, leaving boxes of empty tobacco tins, gin bottles and wireless batteries, etc.

We were shown the hole and deposited our treasure on top of a sundry assortment of farm rubbish and many carcasses of dead sheep.

Still visible above this spoil was a well-constructed brick wall. What was it? I was interested. I took the first opportunity to ask Mr. Stewart at Grange Farm. He told me it was a cellar of an old inn that stood on the roadway to Northampton. This satisfied me for the time being, but I had my doubts.

A hundred yards above the hole is a well in fine condition, not of great age, discovered when the field was ploughed from its old ridge and furrow; also, there were large amounts of animal bones; sheep and cattle, and lots of fragments of Victorian pottery and clay pipes.

The foundations of two long buildings could also be seen. It became apparent to me that this was the remains of an encampment for railway navies, being adjacent to the large embankment, the centre of the construction of the railway. Much of their debris would have gone into the hole; from the amount of meat bones the workers would seem t have been well fed.

Looking through the archives of the Throckmortons at Weston Underwood, we found letters referring to explorations in 1667, when drift mines were dug in search of coal. Only in Hill Field was good coal found and the area can be identified but was abandoned because of flooding.

Could our hole be another mine? It seems unlikely as in the list of materials supplied by the estate to the venture, there were no bricks, leaving us to believe, as there had been limestone extracted on the next hill, it was probably a kiln, most likely Roman.

Post War Cricket at Weston Underwood 1946

There was great enthusiasm in 1946 to reform the Cricket Club.

I attended a meeting in the Park with about ten others. We had permission to use the square laid down in 1900. Our first task was to find it, where years of long grass and animals had covered it. Concrete bases were found for the fence and cleaned out. The fence itself was found in Mr. Graves' farmyard, the oak posts and wire still in good condition.

The square was poor, weedy and rough. Our roller made little impression but we assembled for our first game; John Hobley, looking quite ill with jaundice home from the Far East, Ron Paybody from a Japanese prison camp, Stan Clarke from Burma, wearing is army tropical trousers he had bleached white (not very successfully), a few others back from the war, some of the pre-war time and we youngsters made up the team.

After a few games with mixed results, the roads through Weston were tarred and a heavy roller was parked overnight in Wood Lane – the right approach to the driver saw our cricket square become as good as any locally.

Our first evening game was over at Stoke Goldington in Whitings' long meadow.

Stoke had good cricketers; some played for good local clubs but were playing that night.

It was a game of incidents; my brother Basil swiped the ball as was his way, the ball was lost in the mowing grass and could not be found; the only other one was very old but still hurt as the bruises I received from George Whiting's bowling lasted several days. We made a reasonable score helped by many extras; their bowlers being very fast, their wicket keeper very slow.

When Stoke batted there was soon controversy. Their opening batsman, known as the Sweep, was caught by our wicket keeper but refused to go saying "I weren't out and I ent gooin!" The umpire said "not out" so our captain, Abie Adams, said to carry on.

Just before the end of the game, which Stoke won in very poor light, our fielder, Jack Clarke, made a boundary catch that astonished everyone. Spectators said that he caught the ball in his hat, but the game ended in smiles and off to The White Lion (later The Hollow Tree) for a jolly evening.

Before we left, our captain, a most amiable man, bought the umpire a drink and had a chat about the game and asked why he hadn't given the Sweep out when he obviously was. He said "last autumn when I broke my ankle, he dug all my potatoes up the allotments and brought them down to my house in his truck and wouldn't take a penny. How could I give him out?"

Weston Underwood cricket team, Maurice's brother John middle row left, and Maurice 4th from right

Playing the Merchant Taylor Boys

Boys from the school came to Olney each summer at the end of the school term to help with the harvest. They camped on the school field and used the school facilities.

One year, as the harvest was late, and Sundays were free, their master asked if Weston would play the boys at cricket. They had no kit or clothing but we told them they would be welcome. We had no boys' team but would play anyone available on the day. As it happened both our better players, who had played at university, were available, so we had a good side.

The boys arrived in khaki shorts and shirts looking very young – we knew it would not be a fair match despite Bert Adams who had seen them looking at the bats and doing a bit of catching practice, saying they look as if they can play a bit.

Our side scored 90 – a good score – as the outfield was mowing grass and their bowling better than expected.

I chatted with the players over tea – they seemed at ease with our score, but I knew they would do well to get 20 against our fast bowlers. However, we were soon enlightened, as their first two fifteen-year olds scored 60 before a wicket fell, our only success!

The Lavender Men

At a meeting of the Newport Rural District Council, the ongoing problem of the sewage pits at Stoke Goldington was up for discussion. More complaints had been received from around the area about the acrid smell from the old sand pit on the Weston Road where the local sewage had been tipped for many years.

Councillor Stan Goss, the new Councillor for Weston Underwood and Ravenstone, suggested he supplied a lorry and driver, if the council would find the men to help load. He would have the foul-smelling filth back at Woodlands Farm and spread it on the stubble to be ploughed in. The work would be done on Saturdays. I was the driver with our small Morris lorry. It tipped by a long screw, wound by a handle.

Arriving Saturday morning, I met my fellow workers. They were ex-Londoner Harry Wills from Olney and China White from Lavendon. Both men drove lavender carts round the villages in the week.

We began loading, I with my usual gusto. "Steady up", said China, "this job must last a few weeks". This was because it was double time and they needed the money. I would be lucky if I got paid at all.

Returning after emptying the third load I found the men were washing their wellingtons in the ditch, "Beer time", they said, "would you take us to Stoke?" I had no money, but they would pay if I drove them.

We arrived at The White Lion. I parked the lorry a polite distance from habitation, put my wellies in the hollow tree and joined the men at the bar – in my socks. Mrs. French gave us a cautious but friendly welcome and this became a weekly visit, each one lasting longer. I took some money after the first day, but found I could not spend it, for they said they were getting an additional bonus.

Also, I was not expected to help load, as I was the driver. I did, however, come in for some sarcasm from some people in Weston; some held their noses as I drove through. I spent my spare time elsewhere for a while.

I don't know if my father ever invoiced this work. He made rapid progress in the council, attending meetings in London and Aylesbury, eventually becoming Justice of the Peace.

This, of course, made me keep out of trouble for the next few years!

Family Pictures: A Reformed Character?

Maurice with two of his children, Peter and Chris

Maurice with children and nieces

Maurice in his eighties

Maurice with his wife Joy

Printed in Great
Britain
by Amazon